BY FRANCE GAGNON PRATTE
AND ÉRIC ETTER

TRANSLATED BY LINDA BLYTHE

THE CHÂTEAU FRONTENAC

*One Hundred Years in the Life
of a Legendary Hotel*

ÉDITIONS
CONTINUITE

This book is dedicated to a true friend
of the Château Frontenac,
Claude Pratte.

Canadian Cataloguing in Publication Data

Gagnon Pratte, France

The Chateau Frontenac: One Hundred Years in the Life of a Legendary Hotel. Issued also in French under title: Le Château Frontenac.

Includes bibliographical references.

ISBN 2-9801674-9-5 (pbk.) - ISBN 2-9803575-0-2 (bnd.)

1. Chateau Frontenac, (Quebec,Quebec). 2. Hotels, taverns,etc. - Quebec (Province) - Quebec- History. I. Etter, Eric, 1955- .II Title.

TX941. C43G3313   1993   647.94714'47101   C93-096886-7

This book was published with the financial support of the Château Frontenac to commemorate its one hundredth anniversary.

Project director and author: *France Gagnon Pratte*

Production coordinator: *Louise Mercier*

Research for Part II: *Christine Chartré*

Text for Part II: *Eric Etter*

Revision of French version: *Claude Sirard*

Revision and proofreading
    of English version: *France Gagnon Pratte* and *Linda Blythe*

Graphic artist: *Norman Dupuis*

Cover and contemporary photography: *Brigitte Ostiguy*

(The other photographic credits are given at the back of the book)

Electronic pre-press: *Compélec inc.*

Printer: *Imprimerie La Renaissance inc.*

© **Éditions Continuité**, 82 Grande-Allée Ouest, Québec

Legal deposit Québec and Ottawa - 1993

ISBN: 2-9801674-7-9 (pbk.)   ISBN: 2-9801674-8-7 (bnb.)
ISBN: 2-9801674-9-5 (pbk.)   ISBN: 2-9803575-0-2 (bnb.)

TABLE OF CONTENTS

This history of The Château Frontenac is every bit the brain child of France Gagnon Pratte, its author. France Gagnon Pratte has long held a deep and abiding interest in historical architecture and the Château is indebted to her for her interest.

The Château and the city it graces are inextricably woven together as one.

Robert S. DeMone

Chairman, President & C.E.O.
Canadian Pacific Hotels & Resorts Inc.

For one hundred years now, the Château Frontenac has won the hearts of millions of people — from honeymooners and poets to business people and heads of state. May the magic live on for one hundred years yet to come...

Philippe Borel

Regional Vice President
and Château Frontenac
General Manager

FOREWORD

The Château Frontenac exemplifies more than any other asset the traditions and strengths of Canadian Pacific. Instantly recognizable in photographs, its fabulous site and bold architecture have made the Château one of the great hotels in the world. Over its one hundred year history, the staff of the hotel have reflected its unique characteristics and provided a level of hospitality that has consistently exceeded guest expectations.

Claude Pratte, a valued director of Canadian Pacific for twenty-three years, has been closely associated with the hotel during his lifetime in Quebec City. The new wing of the hotel, to be opened in 1993 and meticulously designed to reflect the heritage of the entire property, has been named the Claude Pratte Wing.

We are pleased that the architectural historian France Gagnon Pratte and Les Éditions Continuité have chosen to honour the hotel with this book as a tribute to its one hundredth anniversary.

W.W. Stinson
Chairman and Chief Executive Officer
Canadian Pacific Limited

Once upon a Time

4. *The Château St. Louis in 1834.*
Engraving by Sproule ANQQ

The First Château:

A SPECTACULAR SITE IN THE NEW WORLD

Once upon a time, there was a castle perched at the top of a steep cliff overlooking a huge, majestic river...

The site of the Château Frontenac was discovered long before the nineteenth century. Its exceptional strategic value was noted by Samuel de Champlain when he was exploring the shorelines of the main rivers in New France, before he founded the city of Quebec. The first fort of Quebec, which housed Champlain's modest living quarters and his sentries, was built in 1620, then rebuilt in 1626. This fort, Fort St. Louis, appears on a 1635 map by Jean Bourdon. The fort contained two wings in addition to Champlain's quarters and was protected by a line of fortification with two bastions. When the first Governor of New France, Charles Huault de Montmagny, arrived in 1636, he began new construction work on the fort and it was named the Château St. Louis.

The construction contract makes for interesting reading:

5. *The Château St. Louis in 1683 by Jean-Baptiste-Louis Franquelin IBCQ*

"Un grand corps de logis et cave pour Monsieur le gouverneur du costé du grand fleuve Sainct Laurens de 86 pieds de long et 24 de large dans lequel il y a cinq cheminées le tout faict de bonne pierre et brique par Lagrange et Louis Robineau Massons et tailleur de pierre tous deux entrepreneurs et ce moyennant le prix de 3150 lb et deux barriques de Vin. Le marchez faict et passé le 24 novembre 1647. (...) Il reste maintenant encore plus de 50 de thoises de l'enclos du fort à faire comprenant la gallerye qu'il faut faire avec la courtine et de plus il faut faire un Corps de Logis pour loger le monde en cas de besoin. Item une boulangerye une prison une citerne et le pont Levy" (Marché pour la construction du Fort de Québec, *Bulletin des recherches historiques*, Vol VII, 1901)

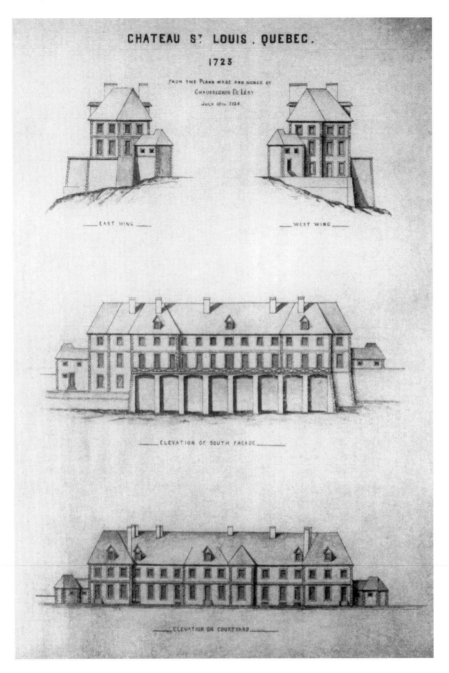

6. *The Château St. Louis in 1723.*
Drawing by Chaussegros De Léry NAC

The Château St. Louis was destroyed on October 16, 1690 when it was attacked by Sir William Phipps, then rebuilt once more on the same site by Comte de Frontenac in 1692. It was damaged by the British at the time of the conquest and had to be repaired in 1764 and 1786. The Château St. Louis burned down on January 25, 1834, although the Château Haldimand, built in 1786 by the Governor-General of Canada Sir Frederick Haldimand, remained standing. Lord Durham had the ruins of the Château St. Louis torn down so that a platform, later to become the city's famous boardwalk, Dufferin Terrace, could be built for the people of the city.

7. "New Chateau St. Louis, Quebec". W. H. Lynn, R.H.A., Architect
Photo: James Akerman, Building News, Oct. 28, 1878

Although it was deprived of its castle for fifty-nine years, the city jealously guarded the site near the Château Haldimand and several citizens submitted reconstruction proposals. In 1875, for example, the Irish architect W. H. Lynn drew up plans which were published in the *Building News*. Fifteen years later, in 1890, the architects Roth & Tilden were commissioned by the founders of a company created to build a prestigious hotel in Quebec City and they designed the Fortress Hotel in the style of the châteaux of the Loire valley in France. Eugène Étienne Taché also drew up plans for the Fortress Hotel in the style of a medieval castle. None of these projects were carried out for lack of funds.

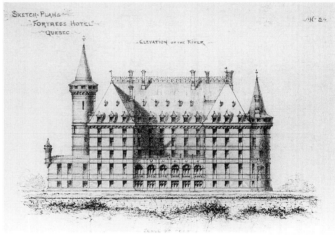

8. "Fortress Hotel", 1890.
Proposal submitted by Eugène-Étienne Taché, Architect ANQQ

For almost three centuries, a long line of people had coveted this strikingly beautiful site. It was one of these, the former French Governor Comte de Frontenac, who was immortalized in 1893 when the new château was built and named after him. The silhouette of the Château Frontenac against the skyline was to become the visual symbol of Quebec City - the cradle of French civilization in North America - despite the fact that it was built by an American architect and its interiors designed by English Canadians.

*9. **Drawing by Bruce Price for the Château Frontenac***
Maxwell Archives, CAC, Blackader-Lauterman Library,
McGill University

PART I

The Birth of the Château Frontenac

Bruce Price, 1892-1899

In 1892, Sir Donald Alexander Smith (Lord Strathcona), Sir William Van Horne, Sir Thomas Shaughnessy and a number of their business acquaintances from Montreal (Richard Angus, James Ross, Edmund Osler, Wilmot Mathews, Sanford Fleming and William Hendrie) formed the Château Frontenac Company in order to finance the construction of a luxury hotel on the site of the historic Château St. Louis. The architect who was chosen by these barons of Canadian high finance was Bruce Price. The hotel was originally supposed to be a contemporary structure but Price's design in the style of a French Renaissance château was truly a masterpiece. Price drew much of his inspiration from the plans drawn up by Taché, Lynn, and Roth &

10. *The Château Frontenac by Bruce Price, as seen from Montmorency Park* C.P.

11. *The Château Frontenac façade on Dufferin Terrace* C.P.

Tilden. In his words: "The motif is, of course, the early French château adapted to modern requirements, a style certainly in keeping with the traditions of the old French city... the materials I believe to be also in harmony with

July 28 '87

W. C. Van Horne Esq.

Dear Sir, I send you by exp. today a sketch and plans for the Quebec Hotel. It seems to me about the thing. The building will give from 175 to 200 rooms and could be built - according to character of finish from $175,000. to $225,000. The material shown is local lime stone and local fine brick with slate roof. The brick are a very good quality good in color and not very expensive.

When will you be in N.Y.? Don't forget to let me know and go to Tuxedo with me. The place is beautiful now after all this rain.

Very truly yours, Bruce Price

13. *Bruce Price drew his inspiration from the châteaux of the Loire valley in France. Château de Jaligny C.P.*

12. *Letter from Bruce Price to W. Van Horne dated July 28, 1887 C.P.*

the surroundings: blue limestone, Glenboig brick, hard, coarse materials, giving broad effects, with plenty of light and color. The hotel is placed in the centre of a big landscape, and hence needs every advantage of bigness, both from the materials and from the simplicity of its designs" (Barr Ferree, "A Talk with Bruce Price", *The Architectural Record*, June 1899).

The American architect even travelled to Saint-Germain-en-Laye in France, the home of the Comte de Frontenac, Louis de Buade. The Château Frontenac, designed by Bruce Price and built by Félix Labelle, was shaped like a horseshoe with a magnificent courtyard in the centre. The main entrance in the courtyard was reached through an arch of stone supported by colonnades. There were four wings of different sizes which housed the rooms and bedrooms and the towers connecting these wings contained the suites. On December 18, 1893, the day the Château Frontenac opened, the *Quebec Morning Chronicle* reported:

"Beyond the shadow of a doubt, the finest hotel site in the world is that now occupied by the Château Frontenac (...) The roofing throughout is of copper (...) the turrets and towers lend to the whole structure the appearance of a mediaeval castle perched upon a precipice (...) Once in the vestibule the visitor is at once struck with the beauty of the mosaic stone flooring and the richness of the woodwork and mural decorations (...) the carved oaken mouldings (...) the grand staircase (...) the arms of Frontenac (...) Frontenac and

14. *The regiment of the Duke of Connaught at the main entrance of the Château Frontenac, 1911 NAC*

Montmagny are each represented in complete armor...".

Over a large marble fireplace in the Coffee Room on the first floor was Quebec City's crest *Natura fortis, Industria Crescit*. The walls of the dining room directly above it were adorned with rare tapestries illustrating the founding of Rome. The hotel's interior was lavish and elegant. Three suites had been designed for very prestigious guests: the Habitant Suite in early French Canadian style, with bright homespun fabrics, *catalognes* and heavy hewn diamond-point cupboards, which paid tribute to the province; the Chinese Suite, with oriental *objets d'art*, which announced that the Château was the first stop after Europe in the Canadian Pacific's route to the Orient; and the Dutch Suite, with Delft tiles and Flemish pictures and furniture, which was designed by Bruce Price in honour of the Dutch ancestry of Sir William Van Horne and the Amsterdam shareholders who had supported the hotel company.

16. *Interior spaces in 1919. Postcard collection* Maxwell Archives, CAC, Blackader-Lauterman Library, McGill University

The hotel contained one hundred and seventy rooms. All of them had open fireplaces and ninety-three had private bathrooms with marble fixtures. The interior design and oak furniture were in the sixteenth century style reminiscent of European châteaux.

15. *Grand staircase in the lobby with the arms of Frontenac to the right* ANQQ, Livernois Collection

17. *A guest room in the Château Frontenac, 1894. Postcard* ANQQ

Bruce Price oversaw the construction and interior design and decoration of the Château himself and kept a keen interest in the smooth operation of the hotel, as attested by several letters.

18. *Model of the first bedroom doorknobs, made by P.&F. Corbin, 1893* Donald Dion Collection; Photo: Brigitte Ostiguy

19. *The Château Frontenac lobby, referred to as the Rotunda. 1906 postcard* ANQQ

The Château Frontenac, along with the Banff Springs Hotel in the Rockies and the Empress Hotel in Victoria, established the château style for the Canadian Pacific. As soon as it was built, the grandiose Château fulfilled Van Horne's promise to make it "the most talked-about hotel on this continent".

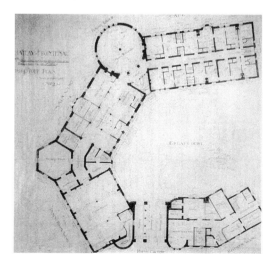

T.G. Shaughnessy Esqr.
Dear Sir, I have been thinking over the conversation we had together with Mr. Van Horne yesterday and hand you this memoranda of how the subject works out in my mind in re Frontenac.
No menu cards except for Dinner.
To effect this properly, bring the service up to the mark of the service in the St. James club and conduct it on the same principle. Therefore have the men in livery, no vests, green cut aways and metal buttons, and pumps; and train them and drill them like club servants.
Let the tables in the Dining Room arranged differently. i.e. take the service trays away from the windows and put guests tables in their place. This space is too valuable and attractive for dirty dishes. Have serving tables like those in St. James club Dining Room in four places (say) in the body of the room.
Does not this seem to be the spirit of the Frontenac.
Yours truly Bruce Price

20. *Letter from Price to Shaughnessy, January 1894 C.P.*

Its asymmetrical design was marked by towers, dormers, steep copper roofs and walls of handsome Scottish brick lightened by the rich grey *Lachevrotière* stone of its foundation walls, turrets and cornices. The novelist Max Pemberton summed up world opinion when he wrote that Quebec was the most beautiful city in the world, and that the Château Frontenac was "a great hostelry like no other one can name - majestic in the fashion of a medieval

fortress, yet as up-to-date as any hotel in America and more comfortable than most". He went on to say: "See Naples and then die! Rather, see Quebec and find a new inspiration to live".

22. *Bruce Price added a wing to the western side of the Château Frontenac in 1899 C.P.*

Right from the start, the Château was an extraordinary success. Although the Canadian Pacific did not attract Europeans initially, the company's American and Canadian clientele enabled it to make impressive profits as early as 1898. In fact, the demand was so great that Bruce Price was asked to design two additions, the Citadel Wing and the Citadel Pavilion. The new wing closed off the horseshoe-shape of the original design.

21. *Bruce Price's floor plan, 1892-1893 C.P.*

With this project, the façades were treated differently. Price abandoned his earlier picturesque details in favour of a much simpler design extenuated by two-storey dormers. This was to be Bruce Price's last addition as he died just a few years later, in 1903.

23. Prince of Wales Suite, 1923 C.P.

25. Dining room, 1919
ANQQ, Livernois Collection

24. The writing room ANQQ, Livernois Collection

Walker S. Painter,
1909-1910

A few years later, the Mont Carmel Wing was added at a cost of one million, five hundred thousand dollars. The architect was Walker S. Painter of Detroit, who also built the Quebec Auditorium (later named the Capitol). Painter's wing - the verticality of its façades, accentuated by tall dormers all the way up to the roof - represented a departure from Price's work. At the end of the northern façade, there was a tower with a sloping roof which was taller than any other building in the old town. This wing was made of reinforced concrete and built by the Provincial Construction Company of Toronto. The addition harmonized beautifully with the rest of the building, and the materials, colours and roofing made up a homogeneous whole with the original structure. With the new wing the Château became the biggest hotel in the country.

27. *The Château Frontenac wing designed by Painter.*
    Poster C.P.

28. *Construction of Mont Carmel Wing,*
    July 2, 1908 C.P.

26. *Dufferin Terrace*
    and Mont Carmel Wing C.P.

29. *Drawing by W. S. Painter for restoration of Château Frontenac, 1907-1909 C.P.*

At the time of his Château contract, Walker S. Painter drew up plans for the Jardin des Gouverneurs which included broad tree-lined lanes. This garden, which was never built, was to be linked to Place d'Armes square by a promenade and was designed to complement and enhance the new wing.

31. *Drawing by W.S. Painter for Mont Carmel Wing, June 1908 C.P.*

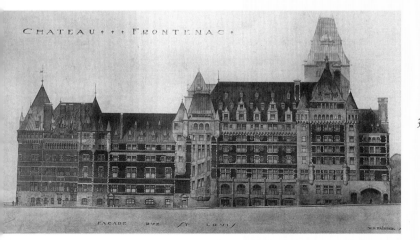

30. *Drawing of St. Louis street façade with Mont Carmel Wing. W. S. Painter, Architect. 1907-1909 C.P.*

33. W. S. Painter's proposal for the Jardin des Gouverneurs, 1909 C.P.

34. Detailed plan for the Jardin des Gouverneurs. W. S. Painter, Architect. 1909 C.P.

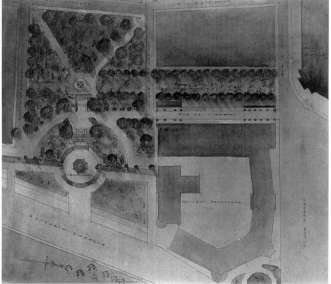

32. Interior design. W. S. Painter, Architect. 1909 C.P.

35. Archway between Mont Carmel Wing and Bruce Price's wing before the 1915 extension C.P.

The 1915 Extension

A few years later, in 1915, the Canadian Pacific decided to remove the arched entrance on the boardwalk side of the hotel, extending the original façade and linking the two wings. This extension was marked by the verticality of its fenestration and by a stone balcony. Last but not least, a lovely new spire roof was built flanked by two corbeled turrets each side of the wall.

36. The 1915 extension C.P.

R A T E S
ACCORDING TO THE
AMERICAN PLAN

FOR EACH PERSON

Room without Bath
per day, $4.00 to $5.50

Room with Bath
per day, $5.50 to $8.00

The range in price is governed by the position of the room.

Baggage is checked at the hotel for all parts of the North American continent served by the Canadian Pacific Railway.

For reservations and information write to

MANAGER
Chateau Frontenac, Quebec.

1912.

37. Rates, 1912
C.P.

La Belle Époque:

THE MAXWELL TOUCH, 1920-1924

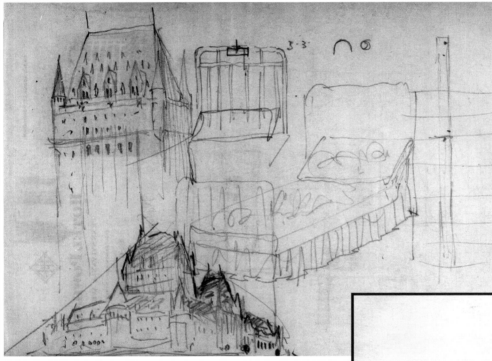

Since 1897, the Montreal architect Edward Maxwell had been designing railway stations and hotels for the Canadian Pacific all across Canada. Sir William Van Horne had also hired the young architect to draw up plans for his summer home on Minister's Island in New Brunswick as well as his farm in Selkirk, Manitoba. Edward Maxwell and his brother William enjoyed a continued association with the Canadian Pacific and Van Horne long after the latter's retirement.

By 1919, rooms at the Château Frontenac were in such great demand that the Canadian Pacific asked the Maxwell brothers to double its capacity. Given the lack of land and the importance of leaving the boardwalk and the Jardin des Gouverneurs intact, the architects proposed the demolition of the service wing designed by Bruce Price and the construction of a seventeen-storey central tower, a new service wing and another wing along St. Louis street. The Maxwells designed their central tower to harmonize with the existing wings, drawing their inspiration from the architecture of the French châteaux of the Loire valley and the tower of Boston's famous Trinity Church designed by H. H. Richardson.

It was a staggering undertaking. To start with, the forty thousand cubic yards of rock in the courtyard that needed to be excavated could not be dynamited because the hotel was occupied by guests. The service wing and western entrance had to be excavated first and the interior courtyard closed off with a slab of cement so that the huge tower could be built.

The tower - an architectural master stroke which unified all the wings - dominated the Quebec City skyline. The wings designed by the Maxwell brothers, like the rest of the hotel, were graced with countless dormers and turrets in the château style. The St. Louis Wing, the interior courtyards and the central tower all meshed beautifully to complete Bruce Price's original work.

The hotel public spaces, offices and lobby - the "rotunda" entered by way of the interior courtyard - were located in the first two floors of the tower. Two grand staircases in the lobby led up to the dining rooms, ballroom, Palm Room and public spaces. Above the dining rooms, the rest of the tower was allotted to guest rooms. There were six hundred and fifty-eight bedrooms in all - eighteen on each floor - which could accommodate a total of one thousand and twenty-four guests. The Château now had twenty suites: sixteen new ones in the tower and the four original ones designed by Bruce Price in the Riverview Wing.

43. *Architectural drawing signed by Edward and W. S. Maxwell* Maxwell Archives, CAC, Blackader-Lauterman Library, McGill University

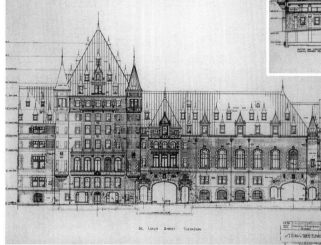

42. *Elevation drawing of the St. Louis façade. Edward and W. S. Maxwell* Maxwell Archives, CAC, Blackader-Lauterman Library, McGill University

Edward Maxwell died before the construction work was finished, and his brother William took over, hiring Gordon McLeod Pitts (1886-1954) to work with him.

The top four floors of the central tower contained suites decorated with seventeenth and eighteenth century antiques and paintings purchased in Europe by Edward Maxwell.

44. *The Château Frontenac as seen from Dufferin Terrace in the Maxwells' day, 1924 C.P.*

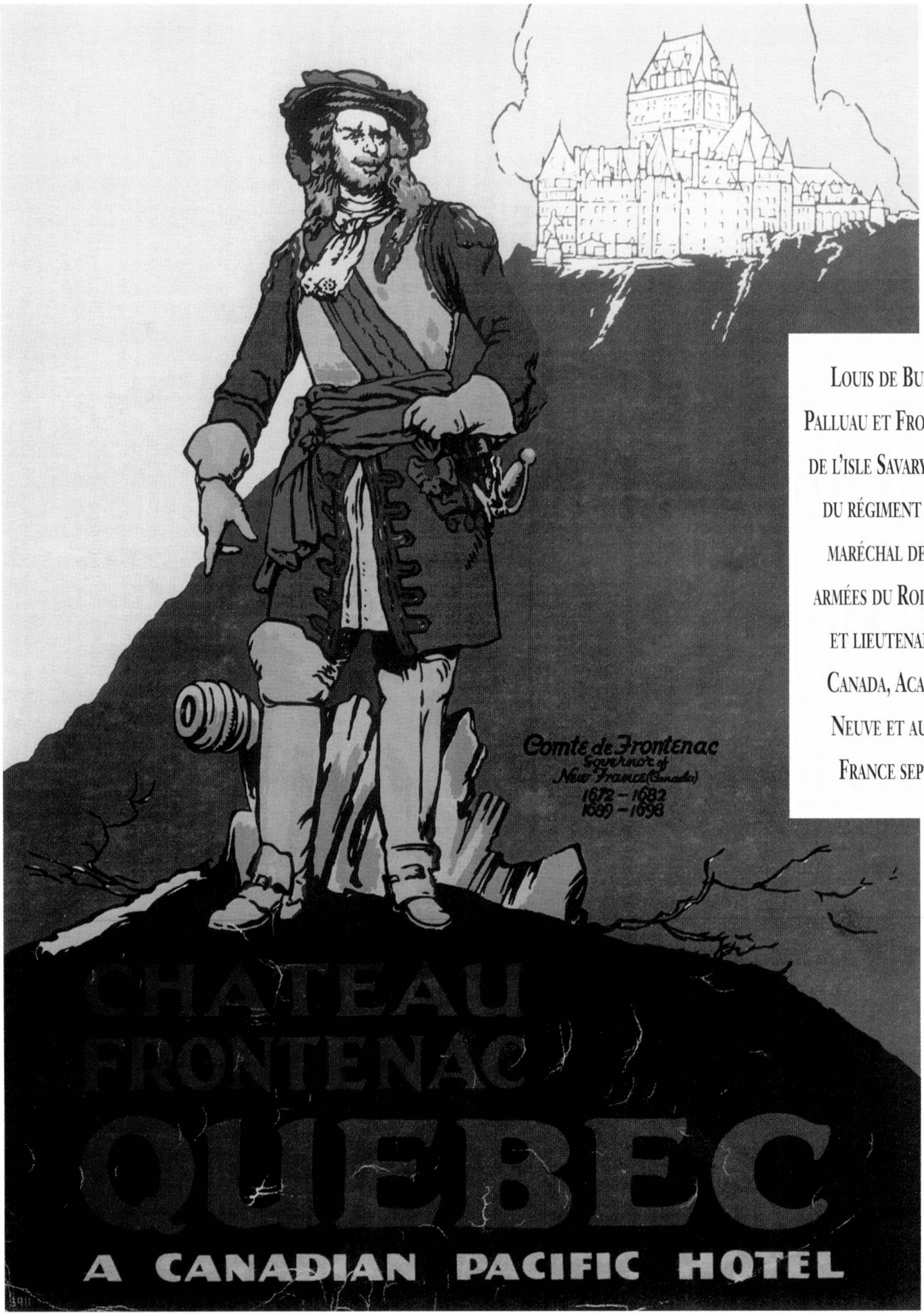

Comte de Frontenac
Governor of
New France (Canada)
1672 – 1682
1689 – 1698

45. *Publicity poster for the Château Frontenac which shows the Maxwell wing* C.P.

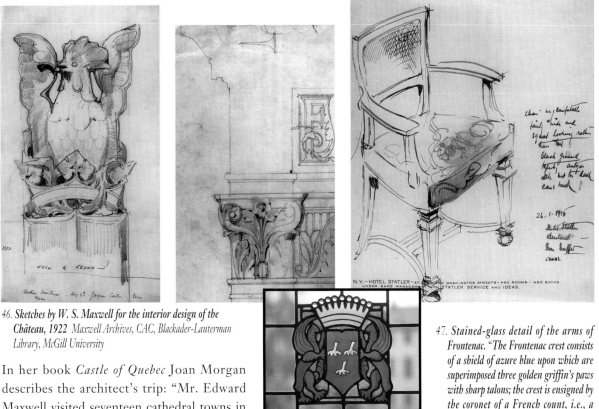

46. *Sketches by W. S. Maxwell for the interior design of the Château, 1922* Maxwell Archives, CAC, Blackader-Lauterman Library, McGill University

In her book *Castle of Quebec* Joan Morgan describes the architect's trip: "Mr. Edward Maxwell visited seventeen cathedral towns in England and almost as many in France. While in Paris he dealt with a firm which was, at that time, the only one in France allowed to remove pieces from the national Museums for reproduction purposes. This was arranged for Mr. Maxwell through the good offices of the great French architect, Violett-le-Duc, then Director-General of Historical Monuments for the French Government. The lists of furniture purchased by Mr. Maxwell on this trip in 1922 are impressive. Jacobean oak bedsteads... Chippendale mahogany bureaux and grandfather chairs... Sheraton mahogany cupboard... Queen Anne walnut writing table and candle stands... Adam rosewood and tulipwood tables... Dutch tortoise-shell mirror and inlaid chair... Louis XV gilt bronze mirror frames.. Louis XIV oak dressing tables... Charles II oak day bed... Cromwellian armchair... Italian carved mirrors...". Each piece had its accompanying ensemble for the room or suite to be fur-

47. *Stained-glass detail of the arms of Frontenac.* "The Frontenac crest consists of a shield of azure blue upon which are superimposed three golden griffin's paws with sharp talons; the crest is ensigned by the coronet of a French count, i.e., a coronet with nine pearls on its short golden spikes. In the Coat of Arms, on either side of the shield, are two winged griffins rampant, supporting it (...)*

A griffin, according to William Cecil Wade's treatise on The Symbolisms of Heraldry, is "a chimerical creature (that) has the head, wings and talons of an eagle, and the body of a lion... Guillim says that it 'sets forth the property of a valorous soldier whose magnanimity is such that he will dare all dangers, and even death itself rather than become captive.' It also symbolised Vigilancy..." Its purpose was to guard valuable treasures, among them the Pearl of Wisdom and the Jewel of Enlightenment, and its kinship was traced, in legend, to the Cherubim who guarded the Tree of Life in Paradise" (Morgan, Castle of Quebec, p 157). *Photo: Brigitte Ostiguy*

48. *Stained-glass window in lobby* Photo: Brigitte Ostiguy

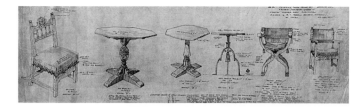

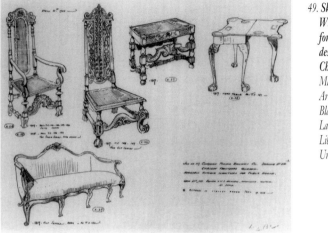

49. Sketches by
W. S. Maxwell
for the interior
design of the
Château
*Maxwell
Archives, CAC,
Blackader-
Lauterman
Library, McGill
University*

Stained-glass windows were much in vogue at the time. William Maxwell designed several for the hotel's public spaces, and stained-glass medallions by C. W. Kelsey depicting such great explorers as Christopher Columbus, Sebastien Cabot and Jacques Cartier adorned the huge lobby windows. The artist Archibald Davies also made stained-glass windows for the hotel, featuring Jacques Cartier, Samuel de Champlain, Le Caron and others.

William Maxwell's private papers in Haifa include many drawings and sketches of wall carvings, furniture, lighting fixtures and even planters and wallpaper for the Château. Many of these drawings were filed with photographs and clippings from architectural journals which had served as inspiration when William was working on the sumptuous decor and furnishings of the hotel. If we agree with the historians that the French Château de Jaligny on the Loire was Bruce Price's model for the Château Frontenac's architecture, then the Maxwells' interior design - with its huge fireplaces, sculpted ceilings, fabulous lights and so on - was inspired by the buildings that William Maxwell studied, numerous sketches and photographs of which are found in his personal files. Among

nished. Thanks to their association with the Arts Club of Montreal, the Maxwell Studio and Canadian artists in general, the Maxwell brothers were able to hire Paul Beau, the artist who produced the magnificent hammered brass and copper pieces, George Hill, one of the most famous sculptors in Canada, and the craftspeople of the Broomsgrove Guild of Applied Arts who made the models for all of the wooden, iron, bronze, plaster and stone ornaments as well as a great deal of furniture for the Château Frontenac wings built between 1920 and 1924.

50. W. S. Maxwell drew his inspiration
for the Château's interior design from
buildings such as the castle of Bracciano
*Maxwell Archives, CAC, Blackader-
Lauterman Library, McGill University*

51. *Interior of the Stowe Westbury house (R.I.), conserved by W. S. Maxwell in his private papers* Maxwell Archives, CAC, Blackader-Lauterman Library, McGill University

them were the Château de Blois, the castle of Bracciano, architectural works in Florence, Bourges and Chartres and a number of stately American mansions.

The Maxwell brothers, and William in particular, worked painstakingly on the details of the hotel's interior design. William's papers include drawings for elevator notices, a special pool table cover for the billiard room and fur-

53. *Sketch by W. S. Maxwell for an elevator notice* Maxwell Archives, CAC, Blackader-Lauterman Library, McGill University

54. *Sketch by W. S. Maxwell for an elevator notice* Maxwell Archives, CAC, Blackader-Lauterman Library, McGill University

52. *Architectural inspiration: library of the Pooler house in Tuxedo, N.Y. Platt, Architect* Maxwell Archives, CAC, Blackader-Lauterman Library, McGill University

niture for public spaces, as well as a sketch signed by William which served as a model for the Palm Room ceiling with its leaf and flowering vine design embellished with cartouches and monochrome motifs. The sketch shows that the artist's palette included many shades of blue against a yellow background. The ballroom was decorated in royal blue and gold. Rich brocades in these colours were draped

over gold curtains and the pale grey hues in the room were picked up by the gilt Louis XVI furnishings. Details of the Maxwell brothers' work were described in a1925 issue of *Construction*. The magazine added: "The beauty of the building, its equipment, the homelike atmosphere and distinction of its service resulted in it becoming known on more than one continent as one of the worthwhile places to visit and linger".

*55. Sketches by W. S. Maxwell for the
Palm Room* Maxwell Archives, CAC,
Blackader-Lauterman Library, McGill
University

*57. Sketch by
W. S. Maxwell
for the Palm
Room ceiling*
Maxwell
Archives, CAC,
Blackader-
Lauterman
Library, McGill
University

*58. The lobby,
1924*
C. P.

56. The lobby, 1924 C. P.

*59. Photograph of
the Palm Room,
as designed by
W. S. Maxwell,
1925* C.P.

60. Hallway, 1993
Photo: Brigitte
Ostiguy

61. *The staircase in the lobby, 1925*
C.P.

63. *Hallway,*
1925 C.P.

62. *Cocktail lounge,*
1945 C.P.

64. *Jacques Cartier Room, 1925*
C.P.

65. *Ballroom,*
1925 C.P.

66. *Staircase at the end of southern*
hallway, 1925 C.P.

67. *Fire breaks out at the Château Frontenac in 1926*
ANQQ, Livernois Collection

Fire and Water:

THE 1926 RECONSTRUCTION OF THE RIVERVIEW WING

Disaster struck on January 16, 1926 when fire broke out in the Riverview Wing. Fortunately, no one was injured and the fire-fighting apparatus of the Château did a good job of limiting the damage. Even though the water froze as it struck the building the equipment worked and most of the hotel was saved. Because of the harsh weather, though, the Château was transformed into a grotesque and distorted ice palace. The fire caused seven hundred and sixty thousand dollars' worth of damage - a substantial amount back then. Almost at once, the Canadian Pacific's directors decided to have the damaged wing rebuilt from Bruce Price's original blueprints. Although nothing concrete remains today of the American architect's orig-

inal building, the spirit of his work has been preserved.

By June, the new wing had been completed by Maxwell and Pitts, and the exterior was a perfect copy of the gutted original. Major

69. Writing room in 1926, after the fire C.P.

68. Writing room before the fire C.P.

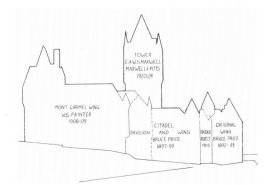

70. Composite plan of the Château illustrating construction phases, 1924 C.P.

alterations were then made to the dining areas, with the Champlain Room being built where the Riverside Lounge had been in the old wing. The spacious Champlain Room was the most outstanding feature of the new wing.

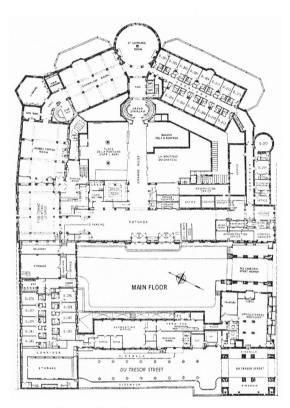

71. *Floor plan of the Château Frontenac, Construction magazine, July 1926* Maxwell Archives, CAC, Blackader-Lauterman Library, McGill University

"The room is carried out with oak piers and large oak beams making twelve ceiling panels (...) These panels have a painted and stencilled design incorporating the British lion and rose with the French griffin and fleur-de-lys, representing the amalgamation of the two races in Canada. A feature of the general treatment is a richly carved oak mantelpiece and panelling nine feet high all around the room (...) The centre panel for the mantel is carved in oak and decorated in color with a representation of Champlain's ship 'Le Don de Dieu' surmounted by the royal French crown (...) The four shields in the frieze carry the coat of arms of Jacques Cartier, de Monts, Charles Huault and La Salle (...) At the tops of the piers there are 34 carved shields bearing the coat of arms of the most important personages including the governors, 'intendants' and others named in the history of New France from the time of Champlain to that of Lord Dorchester (...) The two doorways at each end of the room are especially treated with carved heraldic animals, with the centre feature of two salamanders supporting the royal French crown, and two overdoor panels painted directly on the wood: one, Champlain leaving Honfleur, the other Champlain arriving in New France (...) The painting of the panels is by A. Sheriff Scott, the heraldry by E. T. Adney and the ceiling of the room by James Crocket.

Another interesting room in the new wing is the circular writing-room (...) The ceiling is the principal feature of the room (...) divided into 12 panels (...) each panel containing the painting of a vessel that completes a notable part in the history of adventure and achievement. For instance, one of the paintings is that of Admiral Nelson's Flag ship 'Victory' (...) the vessels in which Cartier and Champlain navigated the St. Lawrence (...) the three vessels in which Columbus set sail from Spain to discover America..." (*Construction*, July 1926).

It took only one hundred and twenty-seven working days from the date of the fire for the new wing to be rebuilt - an amazing feat for the Canadian Pacific and its contractors Anglin-Norcross Limited.

The refined, exquisite interior decoration of the hotel's bedrooms was the work of Kate Armour Reed, the wife of the hotel manager Hayter Reed. For decades to come, her wonderful artistic taste was to mark the château's interior spaces. The Canadian Pacific recognized the quality of Mrs. Reed's work at the Château and later arranged for her to be consulted by the architects when its other hotels were being decorated (Joan Morgan, *Castle of Quebec*). Kate Armour Reed died in 1928 at the age of seventy-two, leaving behind her the legacy of an interior decor that was unmatched in originality.

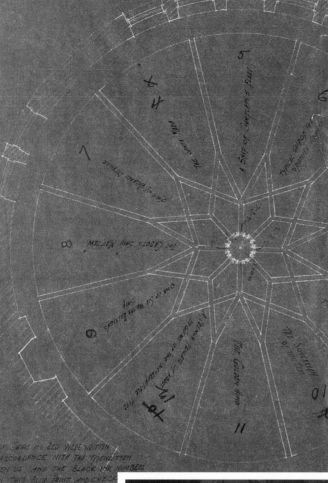

In designing the interiors for the central wing, the Maxwell brothers carried on in the spirit of Mrs. Reed's work, often even using the same colours. With their additions, the Château Frontenac became inseparable from its romantic central tower. The tower was a masterpiece - the crowning achievement that gave the famous Canadian Pacific hotel its international stature. From that point on, it became the most-photographed hotel in the world.

72. *Drawing by W. S. Maxwell for the writing room ceiling built after the 1926 fire; it disappeared in 1992 C.P.*

73. *Lounge across from the Palm Room, 1924 C.P.*

74. *View of the Château Frontenac from Montmorency Park*
Photo: Brigitte Ostiguy

75. *Room 1419*
    in 1925 C.P.

THE CHATEAU
IS REMODELLED
1973

remodelling of all guest rooms, new convention facilities, three new bars, three more restaurants, new air-conditioning in certain parts of the hotel and upgraded heating, plumbing and electrical systems (*CPR Archives*, 1973).

This ambitious renovation program was designed to bring the hotel up to date - certain critics had said that it was stuffy - but it meant setting aside the principles of architecture and interior design that had guided Van Horne, Bruce Price and Edward and W. S. Maxwell. The "new look" of the Château's interior was to change the distinctive aura of certain areas of the building and diminish the elegance and stylishness that had always prevailed. This impact was mostly apparent on the floor which gave out onto the boardwalk, where "a replica of an early French Canadian village" was built which included a new restaurant that was supposed to resemble an old-fashioned kitchen, with open hearths and a bakery, as well as a bar, ice cream parlour, craft workshop and boutiques. The restaurant, named the Café Canadien, stressed the traditional, with French Canadian cooking, pine furniture, diamond-point cupboards, *catalognes* and tile floors. The staff wore period "costumes" that were supposed to look like what country folk used to wear.

76. *Drawing for Grande-Allée proposal by François R. Côté, 1973* C.P.

The original interior design of the Château by the Maxwell brothers has remained, although a number of alterations have been carried out over the years in order to keep the guests coming and reflect more modern tastes. In 1973, the Canadian Pacific announced its plans to make renovations. The Montreal firm Consultants Inc. directed the "restoration program" jointly with the architects Gagné, Bauman & Bouchard, also from Montreal. The general contracting firm was Beaudet, Marquis Enr. of Quebec, and the interior designers were David Williams & Associates of New York.

The general manager, Peter Price, announced that the program would include the

77. Drawing of the Café Canadien by François R. Côté, 1973 C.P.

This restaurant area on the lowest floor was in marked contrast with the refinement and elegance of the rooms just above it. The tile floors, bare walls, pseudo-rustic lighting fixtures, furniture and architectural similarity to the shopping centres growing up in and around Quebec City could not have been less suited to a hotel like the Château.

78. Drawing of the early French Canadian village by François R. Côté, 1973 C.P.

On the main floor, the north/south corridor referred to as the *Grande Allée* was enlarged and remodelled into a "shopping concourse". Its coffered ceiling was covered with a modernistic material pin-pointed with recessed lights. At the south end, the writing room was changed into a two-level cocktail lounge decorated on a nautical theme and enhanced by the Maxwells' original panels of old sailing ships. When the latest restoration work was being done in 1992, these panels, which had been conserved and repainted, disappeared; they were never recovered.

The 1973 renovations also included alterations to the Champlain Room. A mezzanine was added, dividing it into two levels and detracting from its spaciousness. A new "entertainment centre" was opened on the main floor with an adjacent library which was used for private luncheons and later made into a piano bar.

The lobby was also redecorated. Thankfully, the changes were only minor and it retained its familiar, distinctive flavour. The hotel's eighteen suites were fitted with air-conditioners and revamped; quantities of antique furniture were removed from the Château's attics and storage rooms and used for these suites.

Although this two-year, ten million dollar renovation program was designed to give the Château a more contemporary look, the hotel's exterior was fortunately not altered in any significant way: the picturesque building remained true to the visions of Price, Van Horne, the Maxwells and Painter. The most historical rooms were not altered; the wood panelling, stone, marble, brick and other original materials were restored and remained as faithful to the history of the hotel as its chandeliers and fireplaces.

To meet a growing demand for convention facilities, the Canadian Pacific had banquet and conference rooms built. These facilities, as well as the ballroom, some suites for private meetings and a number of shops, were all gathered together on the same floor.

Ten years earlier, the Canadian Pacific had reorganized its hotel division: Canadian Pacific Investments, a subsidiary of Canadian Pacific Limited, incorporated Canadian Pacific Hotels Limited then acquired the Château Frontenac.

Modernized Facilities

At that time, the kitchen took up an area of ninety feet by twenty feet in the centre of the building. The kitchen and its adjoining bakeries and butcher's facilities were just a few steps from the dining rooms. The kitchen manager's office and the cold storage rooms were directly linked to the kitchen by three elevators. An article in the May 1924 issue of *The Contractor* describes the new electric ovens and hot plates which increased the hotel's heating capacity - most of the heating was done with coal prior to that. The article adds that the kitchen appliances were electrical, and goes into considerable detail about the wonders of the power plant and machine room. It is interesting to note that the first electricity produced by water power at Montmorency Falls supplied energy to the Château Frontenac.

The Maxwell additions had been carried out in keeping with the strictest building standards of the day. The reinforced concrete flooring and roof slabs were borne by a structure made of tempered steel. The walls were made of clay blocks, except around the public entrances where gypsum blocks were used as a fire retardant. As for the roof, a skeleton of steel rafters supported the metal lath which was covered with special plaster made up of sand, asbestos and Portland cement, making the roof fire-proof. These roofing materials were covered with copper.

79. The kitchen humming with activity, 1924 C.P.

The hotel was equipped with the latest in alarm systems: fire alarms, a signal board system for chambermaids, switchboards for the head housekeeper, telephones, watchman's clocks and a pneumatic dispatch system. All of this equipment was very sophisticated for the times.

The Château Frontenac was nearing the latest phase of its restoration: that of the 1990s. One must realize that behind the scenes there were all sorts of rooms with equipment and machinery vital to the hotel's operation that also had to be renovated: the machine room and power plant; the water storage room (the tanks in the central water tower held twenty-three thousand gallons, with a total of sixty thousand and five hundred gallons in all the tanks); the hot air ducts; the control room; workshops for carpentry, plumbing, laundering and linen; the accounting offices, staff rooms, canteens and sleeping areas; and of course the hotel's huge kitchens. All of these facilities were modernized under the 1973 restoration program.

80. *Drawing of view from Mont Carmel street. Arcop, 1990*
ARCOP et associés

Keeping the Faith:
THE CLAUDE PRATTE WING
1987-1993

Although the Château Frontenac under-took various renovation projects from time to time after the extensive overhaul in 1973, the building was showing signs of its age. Break-downs were a frequent occurrence, the air-con-ditioning, guest rooms and bathrooms were outmoded, and the kitchens left much to be desired. Although the Château was still the most prestigious hotel around, it was going downhill and did not compare very favourably with the city's new hotels and their elaborate convention facilities, generous parking, swim-ming pools, work-out and recreational facilities and spas.

The Canadian Pacific was hoping to cele-brate the hotel's centennial in grand style before it embarked upon a new era of prosper-ity and excellence. It was therefore essential that the Château be brought up to internation-al standards. On March 2, 1989, the manage-ment of Canadian Pacific Hotels and Resorts announced a sixty-five million dollar restora-tion and renovation program to honour the Château Frontenac's past and prepare it for the future.

These were to be the most extensive alter-ations the hotel had undergone since the Maxwells' day. The Canadian Pacific's priority was to maintain the historical atmosphere and international reputation of the Château Frontenac. The architects were therefore asked

to modernize and introduce sophisticated tech-nology to the Château without detracting from its old world charm and elegance. A team of specialists and consultants spent three months working with the general manager, Gilbert Cashman, and the service heads under him so that they could incorporate their suggestions for improving both the employees' working conditions and the guests' comfort into their plans.

81. Mont Carmel street elevation drawing, Claude Pratte Wing. Arcop, 1990 ARCOP et associés

82. *The Café de la Terrasse, 1992*
Photo: Brigitte Ostiguy

83. *The redecorated Van Horne Suite, 1993* *Photo: Brigitte Ostiguy*

The renovation and construction program took six years, from 1987 to 1993. In 1987 and 1988, the guest rooms in the Mont Carmel Wing, Riverview Wing and the lower floors of the Maxwells' tower were renovated under the direction of Quebec architects Gauthier & Deschamps in cooperation with the general contractors Beauvais & Marquis and Beauvais & Verret. The interior design was done by Alexandra Champalimaud et Associés.

From 1989 to 1993, the Quebec architects Dorval & Fortin, assisted by the architectural firm St-Gelais, Tremblay & Bélanger, restored and renovated the guest rooms in the upper portion of the central tower, the guest rooms in the St. Louis wing, the kitchens, the service areas and basements, the shops along the boardwalk and the entrance exterior.

The architects had access to an abundance of information on the Maxwells' construction work, decoration and design between 1920 and 1924. France Gagnon Pratte, who had done extensive research on the Maxwells for her book on the architecture of Edward and W. S. Maxwell and for a Canada-wide exhibition put together with the other members of the Maxwell Project, had discovered essential information on the Château Frontenac in the shape of nine hundred and fourteen plans conserved at McGill University and numerous notes, drawings and sketches by William Maxwell found among his private papers in Israel.

There is a decided touch of class to the interior furnishings and design by the firm of Alexandra Champalimaud et Associés, especially on the floor which gives out onto Dufferin Terrace. The restaurant, with its big bay windows looking out over the St. Lawrence and the boardwalk, has the refined charm of the main dining room. The former early French Canadian "village" has been replaced by elegant boutiques, an ice cream parlour and a fine luncheonette which can be entered from the outside. Higher up, a conservatory overlooking the boardwalk is reached from the Bar Saint-Laurent, enticing guests outdoors for a stroll. Every one of the five hundred and nineteen bedrooms in the wings have been renovated and the bathrooms have been given marble floors, new ceramic tiles and all the modern comforts.

The most spectacular project to be undertaken has been the construction of a new wing adjoining Painter's Mont Carmel Wing. The architects for this project, the Montreal firm Groupe Arcop, worked with designers from Alexandra Champalimaud et Associés, the contractor Jean E. Verreault et Fils Limitée, structural engineers from Groupe-conseil Solivar and mechanical and electrical engineers from Liboiron, Roy, Caron et Associés.

The architects had considered two options: they could either build a contemporary wing with a modern design and materials or a wing that was in keeping with the existing structures.

It was decided that the new wing would be inspired by the work of the Maxwells and Painter both inside and out so that the new section would blend in harmoniously with the rest of the hotel.

85. Mont Carmel street façade in progress, 1992
Photo: Gilbert Deschamps

86. Gazebo, 1993
Photo: Brigitte Ostiguy

To compete with all the huge, modern hotels now available, the Château needed to be equipped for large international conventions and a wider range of tourists.

The Château now has six hundred and ten guest rooms and four luxury suites, one of which is on two floors. The convention facilities include twenty conference rooms and spaces, with capacity varying from ten to nine hundred. There is also a new suite on the main floor for receptions with a panoramic view of the St. Lawrence. In order to meet the needs of today's health-conscious guests who like to practise sports and do exercises first thing in the morning, the Canadian Pacific has given the Château a health club that includes

84. The conservatory, 1992
C.P.

87. *The Palm Room*
Photo: Brigitte Ostiguy

88. *View of the*
Palm Room
from the grand
staircase
Photo: Brigitte
Ostiguy

91. *The Palm Room ceiling designed*
by W. S. Maxwell
Photo: Brigitte Ostiguy

89. *Detail of Palm*
Room ceiling,
1993 *Photo:*
Brigitte Ostiguy

90. *The Palm*
Room *Photo:*
Brigitte Ostiguy

92. Pool terrace, 1993
Photo: Brigitte Ostiguy

93. Mont Carmel street façade, 1993
Photo: Brigitte Ostiguy

all the latest equipment and an indoor pool giving out onto a terrace and gardens facing the Parc des Gouverneurs.

The interior spaces are all tastefully luxurious, with cherry and maple panelling, plush carpets that one sinks into, elegant lighting fixtures, and antiques and contemporary furnishings created with a mind to gracious living. The tradition of Kate Reed lives on in the interiors created and restored by Alexandra Champalimaud: the designer has avoided any hint of showiness in her marvelous blend of modern comforts and refined charm.

94. *The pool, 1993*
Photo: Brigitte Ostiguy

95. *The Frontenac crest. Detail of commemorative plaque for the Claude Pratte Wing, 1993*

The Claude Pratte Wing on Mont Carmel street has been designed in the spirit of Painter's work. It has steep copper roofs with numerous dormers which blend in with a corbeled turret at the centre of the Mont Carmel street façade. A gazebo at the end of the terrace makes a delightful contribution to the overall picturesque composition. The masonry is particularly well done, with the same contrast Painter adopted to lighten the tall surfaces: the limestone is identical in colour and texture to the stone used for the other buildings and grey stone is used for ornamentation emphasizing the two-storey dormers and for the vertical stone band moulding along the façade.

The new wing bears testimony to the architects' determination to honour the visions of all the architects who have worked on the Château since Bruce Price.

It is this architectural tradition - this continuity - which stands out when one thinks of the Château Frontenac.

96. *Ornamentation designed by W. S. Maxwell* Photo: Brigitte Ostiguy

PART II

One Hundred Years in the Life of a Legendary Hotel

The First Night: In the Wee Small Hours

Imagine that it is late on the night of December 20, 1893 and that the hotel's first guests are returning from the ballroom to their rooms in the Riverview Wing. They have been listening to the *Quadrille du Château Frontenac*, composed for the occasion by Quebec City music teacher Renée Jacques. Try to imagine how they felt, after arriving by train from Montreal, Toronto, Ottawa and the United States and being literally transported into another place, another time. They found themselves in a small corner of North America which, while conceived by North Americans, was reminiscent of Europe, or at least of the castles and opulence of court life on the Continent. Imagine how overwhelmed these distinguished guests would have been by the fabulous decor, and how charmed and sated by the delicious banquet concocted for them by Henry E. Journet, the famous chef whose offerings had already graced the best tables of Paris, London and Amsterdam. Picture them - somewhat tipsy from the vintage wine - trying to fall asleep amidst all this magic, in the wee small hours...

The Red Carpet Treatment

All of the hotel's guests were made to feel like lords and ladies of the manor - or castle! For one hundred years, the entire staff of the Château, from the humblest to the most senior, has devoted itself to the guests, treating them like royalty. This century of hospitality is filled with many interesting and amusing incidents - such a lot of anecdotes to tell! It did not take nearly that long, though, for the Château Frontenac to make a world reputation for itself. In fact, it soon became something of a legend. Right from the start, when it was officially opened in December 1893, the pride and joy of the Van Horne empire was destined to emulate the tradition of excellence of the great European hotels. The challenge was taken up masterfully by all of the hotel's general managers, from H. S. Dunning, the first, to Philippe Borel, the current manager. George Jessop, possibly the most influential of the Château's mentors, managed the hotel for all of twenty-seven years, serving as host to thousands of guests from 1945 to 1972.

It was like the wildest of dreams had become true, and Quebec City would never be the same again. The imposing silhouette of the Château was to become the hallmark of the city and the hotel Quebec City's social centre. What is more, when the future Prime Minister of Canada, Sir Wilfrid Laurier, visited the Château Frontenac in January 1894, he ushered in another great tradition: the rooms, suites, lounges and drawing rooms of the hotel became something akin to back rooms of power. We will never know how many momentous political decisions were made within the hushed confines of the Château, but it is clear that the spirit of the hotel has inspired countless politicians... Thus, at the turn of the century and the meeting point between two worlds - the old and the new - the Château

98. Ornamentation designed by W. S. Maxwell
Photo: Brigitte Ostiguy

Frontenac became the symbol of Quebec's march into the 20th century.

Obviously, the Château Frontenac earned its reputation first and foremost as a great hotel. Right from the start, its philosophy, directly inspired by that of the renowned European hotels, helped build this reputation, which still holds true. The secret of its success can be summed up in these words: the best personalized service. The number of hotel guests grew and grew, and every single person who came through the revolving doors was greeted personally. Their every little desire was immediately seen to. The entire staff, from the general manager to the elevator operator, had only one thing in mind: satisfying the customer. The hotel had to be faultlessly, almost regimentally, organized in order to achieve this end.

This dedication to perfection was also necessary because the Château's clientele, originally mostly from the United States but now from all over the world, was accustomed to the best. Remember, the hotel has always been a favourite of aristocrats, diplomats, heads of state and famous performing artists and business people - VIPs, in other words. These people would not have tolerated poor service for a minute. Then and now, the hotel was run in such a way as to avoid the least little breach of etiquette, and employees were subject to strict codes of dress and behaviour. The same rigour applied, and indeed still does, to all visible and invisible aspects of the services provided: a good reputation is the best form of advertising.

The hotel had to run as smoothly as a Swiss watch, for the Château grew over the years, from one hundred and seventy guest rooms to six hundred and ten. It became virtually a city unto itself. Services have always needed to be organized to perfection, for the Château has as many as six hundred employees during its peak periods.

When you visit the hotel and see the impressive size of the laundry, boiler room, workshops and kitchens, all humming with activity, you realize just how daunting a task it is for the Château to uphold its tradition of quality service. Everything is done on the hotel premises: laundering of linen and guests' clothing; furniture repair; monitoring and maintenance of electrical installations, plumbing, heating and hot water systems; and maintenance of the hotel's two thousand windows, which includes adding a second set every fall since double windows are needed in winter. And this is without counting all the baked goods, pastries, and other tasty items that are prepared for the hotel's restaurants. Also, the thousands of square meters of walls, floors and carpets need to be kept clean.

There are tradespeople of all stripes working at the Château. Behind the scenes, plumbers, electricians, painters, plasterers, locksmiths, tinsmiths, upholsterers, carpenters, welders, laundry workers and needleworkers all contribute to the smooth running of the hotel. When one adds to this list all the service employees who are in direct contact with the guests - reception desk clerks, chambermaids, waiters, wine stewards, concierges and bellhops, to name but a few - one begins to grasp what an enormous organizational undertaking it is to run this huge hotel.

The hotel organization is based on a strict hierarchy, with the general manager and various assistants in charge of well-defined areas of expertise at the top. Their jobs have changed in name only over the years, for they still entail guaranteeing the quality and reliability of the hotel's unique customer service. At present, some of the key people under the general manager and regional vice-president are the hotel manager, assistant manager in charge of restaurant services, sales and marketing manager, customer service manager, hotel accomodation manager, convention manager, controller and head housekeeper, but there are many more.

A Long Line of
Distinguished Servants

Some of the managers who have ensured the smooth operation of the hotel are H. S. Dunning, from 1893 to 1900, Hayter Reed, from 1900 to 1905, Tetlor McMahon, from 1905 to 1919, B. A. Neale, from 1919 to 1928 and 1935 to 1945, and George Jessop, who managed the Château from 1945 to 1972 and upheld the unique philosophy of Quebec's finest hotel. Not only did Jessop establish the Château Frontenac's great reputation once and for all, he also extended its influence by helping to train scores of senior employees who travelled around the world, spreading the special spirit and devotion characteristic of the Château's employees.

*99. Laundry room
in the St. Louis
Wing, 1924
C.P.*

George Jessop was succeeded by Peter Price, who was in turn followed by L.S. Smid, Stanley W. Ferguson, Gustav Bamatter and, between 1986 and 1992, Gilbert Cashman, the first manager of the Château from Quebec City. Philippe Borel is currently running the hotel, now in its hundredth year.

The service records of the different general managers show that they all stayed for fairly long periods, most of them for over ten years and Mr. Jessop for all of twenty-five years! This remarkable loyalty is also evident at the base of the pyramid. In fact, many Château Frontenac employees performed thirty and even forty years of service. Former manager Gilbert Cashman told us that his father Willie and his Uncle Joe accumulated one hundred years of service between them!

Working at the Château Frontenac is not like working anywhere else. Rose-Aimée L'Heureux is a good case in point. Madame L'Heureux retired from her job as assistant to the head housekeeper on March 1, 1993 after a thirty-three year career at the Château. She began as a chambermaid in 1950, was promoted to floor supervisor in 1958, and finally to assistant head housekeeper in 1985. When she started at the Château, she worked non-stop from 7:30 a.m. to 4:00 p.m. one week, then from 9:00 a.m. to 5:30 p.m. the next week, and sometimes "split shifts" from 7:30 a.m. to 12:30 p.m. and 5:30 p.m. to 10:00 p.m. She told us that a strike in 1964 - the only one in the Château's history - led to the shifts being changed. The chambermaid's job is no easy task, with each worker having to clean fourteen rooms, the same number then as today. This gives the chambermaid one half hour only to complete each room. Needless to say, there is no time left over for resting on one's laurels.

Up to the early seventies, chambermaids had to be single and live on the hotel premises. As Madame L'Heureux put it, if you got married your career was over. These young women were subject to strict rules of discipline which included a curfew and not being allowed to receive visitors in their rooms at the Château. Special rooms were placed at their disposal for when their parents came to visit.

Madame L'Heureux admitted to us that in spite of these strict rules she considered herself lucky: the rooms were comfortable, the food was excellent and the salary was good.

Lionel Verret is another good example of employee loyalty and devotion. Presently working with room service, he began at the Château over forty-six years ago and is quite proud of his career there. He earned twenty-eight dollars and fifty-seven cents a week when he started in 1946, and feels that he has always enjoyed good working conditions. The discipline that has been called for in his work over the years has never bothered him at all. It should be pointed out that he is so well known for his engaging and courtious manner, his professionalism and his competence that some hotel guests always ask for him personally. Many celebrities, the famous singer Georges Guétary for one, have even written to him to show their appreciation. In 1990, he received the honour of being chosen Employee of the Year.

Monsieur Verret has fond memories of many activities organized by the hotel for its employees in the course of his years of service. He says that the one he likes the best is the Christmas party, a lively get-together in the ballroom to which the employees' families are invited, to the great joy of countless children whose laughter can be heard from afar.

*100. **Party for the Château's employees; Verret can be seen on the far right as a young man** L . Verret Collection*

101. Lionel Verret: 46 years of loyal service C.P.

Monsieur Verret talked to us with a great show of enthusiasm. He obviously loves his work and always goes about it with a big smile on his face. The idea that he might ever retire does not seem to occur to him.

Monsieur Verret is only one of many people who enjoyed long careers at the Château Frontenac and whose personal and professional qualities contributed greatly to the famous reputation of the hotel on Carrières street.

Royalty, Celebrities, Dignitaries...

The cases of Madame L'Heureux and Monsieur Verret bear witness to the sense of belonging, of being part of a big family, shown by the Château Frontenac's employees. When one meets people like them, one cannot help but believe in the existence of a special Château spirit: an ephemeral stamp that defines this sense of belonging and is often passed on from one generation to the next, weaving a fabric of family-type relationships among kindred spirits - often, in fact, between members of the same family all working at the hotel.

This special spirit is also somewhat akin to the *esprit de corps* found among comrades-in-arms, probably because of the strictly organized work involved which always demands the very best from each and every one. This kind of spirit incites loyalty, and it allowed the Château Frontenac to hang on to its highly skilled employees when large new hotels growing up in the area in the early seventies tried to tempt them to desert.

What is more, this spirit, or devotion, has lived on and even spread around the world since the Château Frontenac has trained countless hotel managers and professionals whose skills are recognized everywhere.

The contribution of the Château's employees to its amazing reputation cannot be denied. In this year of centennial celebrations, each and every one of them deserves to be heartily congratulated.

"An hotel like the Chateau Frontenac is designed for the reception of kings and their retinues, princes, prime ministers and cardinals. But as such important persons do not arrive every day, it is necessary to secure a more stable clientele: American tourists. (...) The authorities of the Chateau Frontenac do their utmost to please this precious clientele. (...) This was the hotel which, that evening, Ovide, stiff as a ramrod in his well-pressed suit, entered with a dazzled Rita Toulouse on his arm. (...) The Chateau was opening its doors to her, bathing her in the glow of its chandeliers, welcoming her to the atmosphere of luxury that her fair beauty deserved and, until now, had been denied. In this sumptuous hall she would receive, so she thought, by general acclaim, the great distinction due to her by virtue of her coiffure, her dress, her shoes, and the locket set with glass beads which she wore around a neck tanned by the summer sun" (Roger Lemelin, *The Plouffe Family*, pp. 278-279).

The Château Frontenac became the most famous hotel in Canada and probably the most photographed hotel in the world. It comes as no surprise, then, that it attracted famous people. Over the past century, celebrated artists and stars from the world of entertainment, politicians, military notables, royalty, financial magnates and many other people of influence and distinction have signed the Château's register.

The future mayor of Montreal, Raymond Préfontaine, was the first to sign, on December 14, 1893, a few days before the official opening of the Château Frontenac. William C. Van Horne, President of the Canadian Pacific Railway Company, who initiated the construction of the hotel, signed the register on December 28, 1893. Sir Wilfrid Laurier, who would later become Prime Minister of Canada, followed suit a few days later, registering *M. et Mme Laurier d'Arthabaska* (Mr. and Mrs. Laurier from Arthabaska - Laurier's constituency) on January 3, 1894.

Right from the start, the Château drew the celebrities of the day, and it has never stopped doing so since. In the century of its existence, King George V, King George VI, Queen Elizabeth as well as Queen Elizabeth II and the Duke of Edinburgh have graced the hotel's royal suites with their presence.

In August of 1919, the Duke of Windsor, who was still the Prince of Wales at that time, the Duke of Kent, Prince Henry and the Dukes of Devonshire and Gloucester, to name only a few members of the royal party, were enthusiastic about the Château's hospitality. The Governors-General and their spouses the Earl and Countess of Aberdeen, the Earl and Countess Gray, the Duke and Duchess of Connaught, Lord and Lady Willingdon, Lord and Lady Tweedsmuir, Lord and Lady Bessborough, and the Earl of Athlone and Princess Alice all stayed at the Château Frontenac in turn in the years before World War II.

The pre-war years also drew other internationally renowned personages. Many World War I heroes, for instance, took advantage of the peaceful atmosphere of the Château to reminisce about their exploits. To name a few, there were French Marshals Fayolle and Foch; Baron Byng, the Commander in Chief of the victorious Allied Forces who distinguished himself at Vimy; and Earl Jellicoe, the hero of the Jutland naval battle.

102. *Queen Elizabeth II with Premier Maurice Duplessis, June 1959 C.P.*

Some of the other celebrated guests during this period were Princess Juliana of the Netherlands, the King and Queen of Siam, Princess Alexandra Kropotkin, British Prime Ministers Stanley Baldwin and James Ramsay MacDonald, Eleanor Roosevelt and Madame Chiang Kai Chek.

But it was in 1928 that one of the most striking apparitions came into the Château lobby. Early on the evening of April 24, Charles A. Lindbergh, the first man to make the transatlantic New York/Paris flight nonstop, strode up to the front desk, complete with parachute. Lindbergh had just flown in from New York - in three and a half hours - to come to the assistance of another famous aviator, Floyd Bennett, who was in a Quebec City hospital with pneumonia. Lindbergh had brought Dr. Thomas B. Applegath with him to administer some special serum ordered from the Rockefeller Institute to Bennett. The patient unfortunately died the following morning.

On the night of his arrival at the Château, Charles Lindbergh was invited by Quebec Premier Louis-Alexandre Taschereau to join him for coffee at a banquet held by the Quebec Garrison Club in honour of J.-Édouard Perreault, the Minister of Colonization, Mines and Fisheries. According to historical accounts, Lindbergh amiably answered all the questions that were put to him by the people at the banquet, who were very interested in the exploits of the American hero.

It was with the Second World War that the Château Frontenac truly acquired international fame, as a result of the Quebec War Con-

ferences in 1943 and 1944. Also, the Duke of Kent was a guest in 1941 and the Earl of Athlone in 1941 and 1946.

After the war was over, heads of state and politicians continued to visit the hotel regularly. In 1947, Princess Elizabeth and the Duke of Edinburgh came to the Château and Canada's Prime Minister Louis Saint-Laurent unveiled a plaque commemorating the two war conferences held there. On June 5, 1954, Emperor Haile Selassie of Ethiopia created quite a stir when he moved in with his retinue of twenty-five which included three Ministers, a porter and four servants. In August of that year, the Duke of Edinburgh made a return visit with his party of twenty-five.

During the 1960s, the number of distinguished visitors grew even more. In September of 1962, the President of Pakistan, Marshal Mohammad Ayub Khan, occupied the royal suite. In February of 1963, Prince Albert of Liège in Belgium came for a visit. The following August, the Lord Mayor of London Sir Ralph Perring and his wife came for a taste of Quebec hospitality. The President of Senegal, Léopold Sédar Senghor, came in September of 1966 to sample the charms of the Château Frontenac.

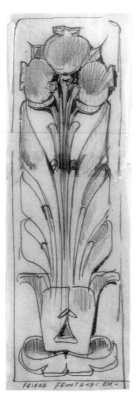

*103. **Ornamentation designed by W. S. Maxwell***
Photo: Brigitte Ostiguy

But it was in 1967, the year of Canada's centennial celebrations and Expo 67 in Montreal, that the Château was to see the most international dignitaries so far.

1 9 6 7

May 5:	Prime Minister Sis Seewoosagur Ramgoolam of Mauritius and his wife
May 10:	Prince Albert and Princess Paola of Belgium
May 12:	Brigadier Tin Pe, Minister of Trade and Cooperatives of Burma
May 15:	President Franz Jonas of Austria
May 17:	President Antonin Novotny of Czechoslovakia
May 24:	President Zalman Shazar of Israel
June 13:	President of the Assembly of Czechoslovakia, Mr. Lastovicka
June 16:	Doctor Doo-Sun Choi, Special Envoy of the President of Korea
June 22:	Prime Minister Dudley S. Senanayake of Ceylon
June 23:	King Bhumibol Adulyadej of Thailand
June 29:	Doctor Zakir Husain, President of India
July 14:	President Asgeir Asgeirsson of Iceland
July 22:	Maurice Couve de Murville, Minister of Foreign Affairs of France
August 2:	Willy Spühler, Vice-President of the Federal Council of Switzerland
August 3:	Doctor Jose Antonio Mayobre, Minister of Mines and Hydrocarbons of Venezuela
August 4:	Prime Minister H. L. Shearer of Jamaica
August 8:	Pierre Mebaley, Minister of the National Economy, Trade and Mines of Gabon
August 10:	Ahmed Senoussi, Minister of Information of Morocco
August 11:	President Grégoire Kayibanda of Rwanda
August 25:	President Félix Houphouet-Boigny of Ivory Coast
August 30:	Prime Minister Rafael Paasio of Finland
August 31:	Doctor Jean-Pierre Lebert, Minister of Economy and Industry of Haïti
September 1:	Prime Minister of Trinidad and Tobago, Doctor Eric Williams
September 14:	President Giuseppe Saragat of Italy
September 22:	Prime Minister E. W. Barrow of Barbados
October 4:	Crown Prince Harald of Norway

The striking General Charles de Gaulle, President of France, also made an appearance in 1967, attending a banquet held in his honour at the Château by the Quebec government. De Gaulle did not pay much attention to protocol, chatting merrily with a wine steward at the hotel and fellow *maquisard*, Henri d'Orange, who was wearing a decoration he had received while serving with the Free French Forces during World War II. Although General de Gaulle had decided not to stay at the Château because of his phobia for elevators, he told the manager Mr. Jessop that the state dinner was the best he had ever been to.

While the quantity of distinguished visitors to the Château went down when Expo 67 was over in Montreal, the quality continued on. In 1969, Princess Grace of Monaco, indisputably the most popular monarch of her time, presided over the Winter Carnival festivities and graced the Queen's Ball with her radiant presence. This Ball was a memorable one indeed, with Pierre Elliot Trudeau dancing with the Winter Carnival Queen!

The heads of state kept coming. The Château received President Elhadj Ahmadou Ahidjo of Cameroon and his wife between September 11 and 13, 1970. A conference was held at the Château Frontenac from September 23 to 25, 1979 by the cabinet ministers of the government of Canada, headed by Prime Minister Joe Clark; there were twenty-three ministers and two senators in the delegation. French Prime Minister Laurent Fabius was Quebec Premier René Lévesque's guest at the Château from November 8 to 10, 1984.

In 1985, two famous men of Irish descent met at the Château to discuss government affairs, also celebrating St. Patrick's Day: Ronald Reagan, President of the United States, and Brian Mulroney, Prime Minister of Canada. Needless to say, the extremely sophisticated security systems and arrangements surrounding the President caused considerable upheaval at the Château and Mr. Reagan's heavily armed security people impressed more than one Château employee!

Early in 1987, the second Francophone Summit attracted dignitaries from French language countries around the world to the Château Frontenac. Once again, the hotel had to cope with special security measures.

In the spring of 1988, on May 11 and 12, the tulips in the Château lobby were particularly radiant when Lieutenant Governor Gilles Lamontagne greeted Queen Beatrice and Prince Claus of the Netherlands.

In mid-July of 1989, it was the turn of Prince Andrew and Sarah Ferguson, the Duke and Duchess of York, to pay a visit. The royal couple announced the winner of the most popular show award at the closing ceremony of Quebec City's International Summer Festival and were introduced to the music of Quebec author/composer/singer Robert Charlebois.

When Queen Margrethe II and Prince Consort Henrik of Denmark arrived at the Château for a state dinner given by Premier Robert Bourassa on October 11, 1991, the direction of traffic had to be changed so that Her Majesty could step directly onto a red carpet as she got out of her car instead of having to go around it.

105. Premier Robert Bourassa and Madame Andrée S. Bourassa at the Château with their guests Queen Margrethe II and Prince Consort Henrik of Denmark, October 1991
Photo: Marc Lajoie, ministère des Communications (Québec)

To add to this long list of notable visitors, there were the American Presidents Theodore Roosevelt, Richard Nixon and Dwight Eisenhower; President François Mitterand of France; Quebec Premiers Paul Sauvé and Daniel Johnson; Prime Minister Jacques Chirac of France; Xavier Perez de Cuellar, Secretary General of the United Nations; and Federico Mayor, Director General of UNESCO.

After Quebec City was named a World Heritage City in 1985, it hosted the First International Symposium on World Heritage Cities, between June 30 and July 4, 1991, with the Château Frontenac at the heart of the city being honoured by an impressive number of mayors from some of the most famous cities in the world.

In the century of its existence, the Château has accommodated dozens of politicians of national and international renown. But we must not forget that it also served as the residence of one of the most colourful men of politics that Quebec has known. Maurice Duplessis, founder of the *Union nationale* party and Premier of Quebec from 1936 to 1939 and 1944 to 1959, virtually made the Château his official home. He lived on the twelfth floor of the central tower and frequently held his cabinet meetings there. One must conclude that many major administrative decisions relating to Quebec were made in the Château Frontenac.

Since Quebec is a capital city, almost all of the ambassadors posted to Ottawa and all the consuls generals stationed in Quebec stayed at the Château when they arrived to take up their post. Most of them insisted on staying there and some would even postpone their visit if necessary until there was room for them.

That's Entertainment!

It was not just diplomatic and political celebrities who appreciated the famed hospitality of the Château Frontenac, however. Scores of artists and entertainers, important business people and sports stars were also charmed by the hotel's unique qualities and atmosphere. A few of the famous French music hall entertainers and singers who stayed at the Château are, in no particular order, Gilbert Bécaud, nicknamed *Monsieur 100,000 volts*; Maurice Chevalier, the singer with the famous straw hat, also renowned both in France and Hollywood for his movie roles; Georges Guétary, the charmer; Charles Aznavour, whose *La Bohème* was probably one of the most moving French songs of all time; Enrico Macias, the Algerian exile who embraced Paris; Tino Rossi, the suave Corsican; Patrick Bruel, the rock superstar from France, who captured the hearts of thousands of teenage girls; Charles Trenet; Yves Montand; Guy Béart; and Michel Sardou.

It would be almost a crime to forget the visit of the legendary Édith Piaf. Among the other illustrious female performers who came to the Château there were Annie Cordy from France and Petula Clark, who charmed the French-speaking public with her British accent.

It goes without saying that many artists and performers from Quebec and the rest of Canada came to the Château Frontenac too: the popular Ginette Reno, the fiery Acadian Édith Butler, the personable Michel Rivard, whose *Complainte du phoque en Alaska* became a classic that everyone still loves to sing along to, and the astounding impersonator André-Philippe Gagnon, a man who could mimic each female and male singer of *We Are the World*, the song composed for the benefit of victims of famine in Ethiopia.

106. Ornamentation designed by W. S. Maxwell Photo: Brigitte Ostiguy

The great jazz pianist Oscar Peterson also made a visit, as did Paul Anka and Tom Jones.

And in case you thought that the Château would not exactly be to the taste of more contemporary pop and rock stars, Chris de Burgh, Cindy Lauper, Bryan Adams and the New Kids on the Block chose it over Quebec City's other hotels.

Quite a few sports stars have been to the Château Frontenac over the years. Boxers Jack Sharkey, Gene Tunner, Jack Dempsey and Rocky Marciano have all stayed there at one time or another. Being a hockey town, Quebec City has drawn many well-know National Hockey League and World Championship players who have stayed at the Château. Such stars of the former Soviet Union's national team as goalkeeper Vladislav Tretiak and the spectacular forward Valery Kharlamov have gone there to rest after certain bitterly disputed games, as have Jean Béliveau, Gordie Howe, Guy Lafleur and Wayne Gretsky of National Hockey League fame. The Château has also hosted the fiery and sorely missed owner of the Toronto Maple Leafs, Harold Ballard, and the entire Harlem Globe Trotters basketball team.

It is only natural that the Château Frontenac, which has always fascinated people, would attract many individuals whose art is fascination - from the worlds of film, theatre and television.

Sometimes it was almost like the Château had been transformed into a Quebec City Hollywood. In 1952, for instance, Alfred Hitchcock moved the prestigious cast of his movie *I Confess* there. Among others, there were stars Montgomery Clift and Anne Baxter, who created quite a sensation when she smoked her big cigars. The hotel staff was also won over by the director himself, who was noted for his healthy appetite and given to ordering incredibly fat steaks several times a week. A few of the movie scenes were shot at the hotel in which the manager Mr. Jessop played himself. Some Quebec actors also got their place in the film credits: Ovila Légaré, Carmen Gingras and Renée Hudon, a popular ten year old radio and television personality who played one of the main witnesses in a murder trial. The world première of the movie was held at the Capitol Theatre in Quebec City in 1953.

There was more excitement at the Château in March of 1969 when it became the headquarters for another movie - *Don't Drink the Water*, based on a story written by Woody Allen. For three weeks, Quebec was the capital city of "Vulgaria", a mythical country somewhere east of what was then called the Iron Curtain. The Château lobby, where several scenes were shot, was sometimes hard to recognize what with all the technical paraphernalia installed there. The star of the movie, the famous Jackie Gleason, attracted a crowd of curious onlookers, which gave the hotel security manager Roland Forget more than a few headaches. It was no easy task trying to protect the movie star's privacy tactfully and hold the enthusiasm of his fans at bay. The hotel management did everything possible so that the shoot could go smoothly, even going so far as to satisfy Jackie Gleason's penchant for Chinese food! The general manager, Mr. Jessop, turned down the part of Gleason's stand-in which the director offered him, however. Another superstar of the movie world visited Quebec during this period and met Jackie Gleason at the Château: Anthony Quinn, the hero of Fellini's *La strada* and the actor who played the unforgettable lead in *Zorba the Greek*.

The names of the scores of other motion picture stars who have stayed at the Château Frontenac over the years are bound to bring back memories to movie buffs. Some of the better known ones were legends in their day. There was Boris Karloff, immortalized for his role as the monster created by Doctor Frankenstein; the handsome Errol Flynn, famous for his warm-hearted, swashbuckling adventurer roles such as Robin Hood; and Bing Crosby, who still thrills millions of listeners and spectators when he croons *White Christmas*. And that is not all. Among the men, there were James Cagney, Conrad Veidt, Ben Turpin, Douglas Fairbanks Sr., Ramon Navarro, Don Ameche, Monty Wooley, Beau Bridges, Walter Pidgeon, Glenn Ford, Raymond Massey, James Garner, Allan Ladd,

Jerry Lewis and Brian Aherne, representing pretty much all the different types of movies ever produced by Hollywood.

This picture of Hollywood notables who frequented the Château would obviously be incomplete without the names of the female movie stars who honoured the hotel with their presence: Jeanette MacDonald, Lily Pons, Barbara Lamarr, Nancy Carrol, Louise Fazenda, Grace Moore, Barbara Stanwyck, Joan Bennett, Shirley MacLaine, Joan Crawford, Jane Seymour, Brooke Shields and Elizabeth Taylor.

Several French actors also crossed the Atlantic to give us a taste of their talent and revel in the creature comforts of the Château Frontenac. For starters there was the divine Sarah Bernhardt, member of the *Comédie-Française* and unquestioned queen of the Parisian theatre scene at the turn of the century. Somewhat more recent visitors were Philippe Noiret, who was made famous by the role of *Alexandre le bienheureux*, and Gérard Depardieu, the prolific actor who became an international movie star after his brilliant Cyrano de Bergerac and memorable Christopher Columbus.

There were also television celebrities at the Château. Among those who stayed there are Joan Lunden, host of the American station ABC's *Good Morning America*, and the popular Michel Drucker, whose variety shows feature all the big contemporary names in French show business.

In addition to providing the decor for a number of movies and television shows, the Château also inspired the French writer Frédéric Dard who, after staying there, decided to use the old city and immediate surroundings of the hotel as the locale for much of his crime novel *Ma cavale au Canada*, which was published in the late 1980s. Frédéric Dard was the creator of the famous police superintendent *San Antonio*, the hero of almost one hundred and fifty books. Dard seems to have been very impressed by the Château's employees because some of them are named and used as characters in his book.

One might expect all sorts of anecdotes to have been generated by the presence of so many celebrities at the Château Frontenac, but actually not all that many stories have "leaked" out. This is really quite understandable given the impressive discretion of the hotel's employees - one of its greatest qualities.

The Discreet Loyalty
of a Château Aficionado:
Edmund Leonard

To conclude this section on all the notables who made the Château their home at one time or another, we would like to say a few words about a man who, although not a celebrity in any true sense of the word, holds the record for the longest stay at the hotel: Edmund Leonard, who lived in his suite there for twenty-nine years, from 1942 to 1971. Leonard is really part of the hotel's history. His parents were among those residents of Quebec City who had had the privilege of attending the opening banquet in 1893. A few years later, in 1902, as he was sitting down to a family dinner at the Château, the young Edmund froze at the sight of an imposing figure with a moustache. He had just caught a glimpse of Theodore Roosevelt, the President of the United States. Forty years later, just after he had moved into his own suite in the hotel, he was to see another Roosevelt - Franklin Delano, or FDR, this time.

108. Drawing by W.S. Maxwell for the interior design of the Château Frontenac
Maxwell Archives, CAC, Blackader-Lauterman Library, McGill University

109. *The 1944 Quebec War Conference. Mackenzie King, Roosevelt, Churchill and chiefs of staff* C.P.

Prelude to Victory:
The Quebec War Conferences

While most of the events that marked the history of the Château Frontenac were festive occasions, the two most important ones were associated with the worst armed conflict the world has ever known: the Second World War.

In 1943, at a point when the outcome of the war was still far from determined, the heads of state of the principal Allied democratic nations decided to meet in Quebec City in the month of August. After the Casablanca and Atlantic councils of war, the British Prime Minister Winston Churchill, United States President Franklin Delano Roosevelt and Canadian Prime Minister William Lyon Mackenzie King decided that another tripartite conference was called for to ensure the success of the coming military campaign. The only building that could accommodate a meeting of this magnitude was the Château Frontenac.

The first indication of the conference came abruptly when the manager Mr. Neale was ordered to cancel all of his appointments for the evening of July 31 for an emergency meeting with Mr. Coleman, the President of the Canadian National Railway. When Mr. Coleman arrived on that date, he was accompanied by his brother, the Under-Secretary of State. Mr. Neale was informed that the Château had been requisitioned by the Canadian government for a period of two weeks or more, starting on August 8. The premises were to be completely evacuated to make room for all the officials and support and security staff of the countries concerned and the reason for this was to remain absolutely secret - no easy accomplishment! With the exception of three people, the eight hundred and forty-nine guests and permanent residents of the hotel had to vacate their rooms and suites by August 6. This inevitably gave rise to numerous arguments and called for a great deal of diplomacy on the part of the management, since the real explanation for the evacuation could not be revealed beforehand. As if this were not enough, some two to three thousand reservations had to be canceled. The only three people who were allowed to stay were the manager, Mr. Neale, his wife, and Lucien de Celles who was moved to their apartment and allowed to stay because of his age. Even the former Quebec Premier, Maurice Duplessis, was turned down when he asked for permission to remain.

In the early morning of August 8, the invasion of the Château by nearly seven hundred people began. For obvious reasons of security, each and every room was inspected and the past of each employee examined thoroughly. The security personnel - from the RCMP, FBI, Provost Corps and Royal Marines - worked twenty-four hours a day. Anti-aircraft guns were installed along Dufferin Terrace near the Samuel de Champlain monument and a squadron of fighter planes - Spitfires - remained on alert at the Lorette airport. A complex system of passes was implemented, with different coloured passes allowing different types of access to the people using the Château during the conference. The hotel staff members were given pink passes. The security measures were so strict that if employees forgot to take their pass with them when they left they could not get in again the next day!

Every room was accounted for. The American delegates were assigned to the even-numbered floors from the sixteenth floor down and the British, to odd-numbered floors from the fifteenth floor down. The fourth floor was reserved for the Canadian government officials and the third, as conference space. Most of the rooms were altered or rearranged to meet the special needs of their temporary occupants, which must have dismayed some of the permanent residents who use their own furniture.

The preparations were completed in time for the hotel's important guests. As an added safety measure, the three chiefs of state were to stay in the Citadel. The Château management was entrusted with the responsibility of setting up their quarters, however. On Tuesday, August 10, the whole world learned that a major conference that could alter the course of the war was taking place in Quebec City. Winston Churchill arrived with his wife and daughter Mary, as his military aide. On August 11, preliminary conferences began at the Château between British and Canadian chiefs of staff. On the twelfth, Churchill paid a visit to the Premier of Quebec, Adélard Godbout, while highranking officers of the United States military arrived by plane and by train. On the thirteenth, the Royal Air Force hero and most-decorated man of the war, Wing Commander Guy Gibson, arrived and - surprise, surprise - Churchill and his daughter left the city for an unannounced destination. On the fourteenth, the grapevine reported that Joseph Stalin of the Soviet Union would be taking part in the conference. The rumour was promptly refuted, and the newspapers announced that Churchill was at Niagara Falls. On the fifteenth, the British Prime Minister returned to Quebec and announced that he had been conferring with President Roosevelt at the latter's residence in Hyde Park. On August 16, the Washington press gallery corps arrived, and President Roosevelt the following day. The conference could then begin.

Meanwhile, the people of Quebec City waited at the arched entrance to the Château, hoping to spot one of the heads of state.

The conference participants spent their days deliberating and their evenings socializing at sumptious receptions and banquets, for which the chefs Louis Baltera and Leonard Rhode were congratulated by Winston Churchill himself. One of the most noteworthy events was a banquet given by Mackenzie King for five hundred and ten people!

The kitchen staff had to work even harder than usual during this busy period. Approximately two thousand meals were served every day, which amounted to over thirty-five thousand meals over the course of the conference. The traditional teatime was kept up every day at 4:00 p.m., with two hundred afternoon teas being served to the dignitaries and their staff.

The key importance of this first war conference in Quebec is borne out by the list of delegates present. Important though they were, they still needed to present their passes at the door before being allowed to enter the Château. From Great Britain, there were Anthony Eden, Secretary of State for Foreign Affairs; Sir Alexander Cadogan, Under-Secretary of State for Foreign Affairs; Lord Leathers, Minister of War Transport; General Sir Alan Brooke, chief of Imperial General Staff; Admiral of the Fleet Sir Dudley Pound, First Lord of the Admiralty and Chief of Naval Staff; Air Marshal Sir Charles Portal, Chief of Air Staff; Vice-Admiral Lord Louis Mountbatten, Chief of Combined Operations; Lieutenant-General Sir Hastings Ismay, Chief of Staff to the Minister of Defence; Sir John Dill, the Washington representative of Chiefs of Staff; and Brendan Bracken, Minister of Information.

The American delegation was pretty impressive too. It was headed by Cordell Hull, Secretary of Foreign Affairs, and included H. L. Stimson, Secretary of War; Admirals W. D. Leahy and E. J. King; General G. C. Marshall, Army Chief of Staff; General H. H. Arnold, Army-Air Forces Chief of Staff; and dozens of highranking army, air force and navy officers.

Canada was represented at the Conference by Colonel J. L. Ralston, Minister of National Defence; Major C. G. Power, Minister of National Defence for Air; C. D. Howe, Minister of Munitions and Supply; T. A. Crerar, Minister of Mines and Resources; J. L. Ilsley, Minister of Finance; J. E. Michaud, Minister of Transport; L. S. Saint-Laurent, Minister of Justice; and many more dignitaries and members of the military.

Other people of importance who attended the Conference were China's Foreign Minister, Dr. T. V. Soong, General Laverick of Australia, Sir William Glasgow, Australian High Commissioner to Canada and, of course, Canada's Governor-General the Earl of Athlone and his wife Princess Alice.

The daily hotel bill for these illustrious guests amounted to eight thousand dollars - one half of the total cost of the Quebec Conference, which was paid for by the Government of Canada.

Winston Churchill should perhaps be given the honour of concluding this section on the first War Conference in Quebec. In reference to his stay, he said in a radio broadcast on August 31: "Certainly no more fitting and splendid setting could have been chosen for a meeting of those who guide the war policy of the two great western democracies at this cardinal moment in the second world war than we have here in the Plains of Abraham, in the Chateau Frontenac and the ramparts of the Citadel of Quebec from the midst of which I speak to you now".

A second War Conference was called in Quebec, and thirteen months later the same players gathered once more. The Château Frontenac was only occupied for ten days this time, however. Although the social events were less elaborate and extravagant, security measures were every bit as strict!

This was not the end of the conferences, though. In early November of 1945, just after the war had ended, representatives from the thirty-one member countries in the newly created United Nations Organization met at the Château Frontenac and signed the charter of the Food and Agriculture Organization (FAO), whose headquarters have been in Rome ever since.

It was with these three conferences, which played such an important role in history, that the Château Frontenac truly gained worldwide renown.

Countless federal-provincial and interprovincial conferences have also been held at the Château over the years.

110. **The Château**
in a snowstorm
Photo: Brigitte Ostiguy

The Exotic North:

WINTER SPORTS AT THE CHATEAU

In addition to being a season marked by all sorts of festivities, winter at the Château is the source of its trademark role as a winter sports centre. In fact, it is largely to the Château Frontenac that Quebec City owes its reputation as "snow capital".

As early as 1894, the hotel played an important part in organizing the Winter Carnival, which the people of Quebec City had decided to take on when Montreal stopped hosting the event. From January 29 to February 3 of 1894, the streets and parks of the city hummed with activity. There were hockey tournaments, skating contests, canoe and snowshoe races, parades complete with extravagant floats, curling and ice hockey competitions, sleigh rides, tobogganing and sledding events, storming of the ice fort by Huron and Montagnais competitors in snowshoes, musical extravaganzas, a grand concert at the Manège militaire drill hall, a fancy dress ball at the parliment and fireworks to thrill local and visiting onlookers. The major buildings of the city, the Citadel and Dufferin Terrace were decorated and lit up and toboggan runs were set up at various locations. An ice fort was built and ice sculptors demonstrated their skills by creating statues which recreated great moments in Quebec history.

111. Canadian Pacific poster, 1926-1927 C.P.

The honorary sponsor of the Winter Carnival, Governor-General Lord Aberdeen, was present for the occasion. The carnival was highly organized, with an executive committee and eighteen subcommittees dealing with accommodations, railways, the press and contributions, among other things. While we are on the subject of contributions, the Château Frontenac was second on the list of key sponsors that year. The City of Quebec, with its generous donation of one thousand dollars, was first. It was followed by the Château, then by J. B. Laliberté, the owner of Quebec City's first department store, each of whose contributions were in the order of five hundred dollars. The President of the Canadian Pacific Railway Company, W. C. Van Horne, donated two hundred and fifty dollars.

Visitors from outside the city were encouraged to participate in the Carnival. According to the official program of activities for the 1894 Winter Carnival, people taking the train from New York to Quebec City needed to allow twenty hours for the trip! The program also pointed out that it took sixteen hours from Boston, eighteen hours from Toronto, six hours from Montreal and all of twenty-four hours from Halifax. Visitors from out of town could stay at the Château Frontenac or at any of the other hotels - the St. Louis, Florence, Royal Victoria, Blanchard, Henchey, Quebec, Chien d'Or or the Mountain Hill House.

The city held another Winter Carnival in 1896 but it was to be the last one for a long time - until 1950.

The Château was a groundbreaker in that it promoted winter and winter activities in its advertising well before the advent of mass tourism. In 1929, a pamphlet entitled *Winter Sports in Old Quebec - Our Lady of the Snows*

112. Canadian Pacific poster "Winter Sports in Old Quebec" C.P.

extolled the virtues of the various winter activities offered by the hotel.

The pamphlet tells us that Jack Strathdee was the hotel's Winter Sports Director at that time and offers such sports as skating, curling, snowshoeing and, for bigger thrills, ski jumping, bobsledding (using equipment imported from Switzerland) and of course tobogganing down the Château's special slide that whisked enthusiasts down the hill from the Citadel, along Dufferin Terrace and right up to the

113. Cocktails on the skating rink, 1945
C.P.

doors of the hotel. Even back then, this famous toboggan run, which has just been restored and reopened to commemorate the one hundredth anniversary of the Château Frontenac, allowed enthusiasts to go over seventy kilometers an hour.

Another activity described in the pamphlet is dogsledding. The idea of forming a dogsled team originated in 1921 and was put into practice the next year. According to Château Frontenac Huskies, published by the Château in 1927, its dog team caused quite a stir among visitors exploring the streets of Old Quebec. Although the dogs were chosen very carefully, they were not meant to take part in competitions, but rather to offer the Château's guests the excitement of a race that was like something out of a Jack London novel.

The driver of the dog team was Arthur Beauvais, an Amerindian from Kahnawake with over fifteen years of experience. His rapport with the huskies was such that he never had to use his long snakeskin whip. The lead dog was named Mountie, and Jeff, Hooch, Smarty, Buster, Wabaska, Husky, Fang and Smoke made up the rest of the team.

Even though the Château Frontenac did not enter its dogsled team in competitions, Quebec did host one of the most famous derbies back then, the *Eastern International Dogsled Derby*, a one hundred and twenty mile event that featured contestants from all over the United States and Canada. Many reporters stayed at the Château and used it as their headquarters.

*114. The Château Frontenac
slide, circa 1929 C.P.*

In a very short space of time, the Château Frontenac made a name for itself among winter sports fans and kept enhancing its services tailored to this clientele.

In the 1930s, curling enthusiasts could practise their favourite sport in the Palm Room, right inside the hotel. For skiers, there were skilled instructors, many of whom were from Switzerland, Germany and Austria, to help them tackle the downhill slopes on the Plains of Abraham, just a few minutes' walk from the hotel. The Château also had a ski shop where skis could be rented and repaired. There was a rink beside the hotel for those who prefered skating, with an instructor on hand for beginners.

There were also figure skating pageants and hockey matches between local teams competing for a trophy offered by the Château. Another famous trophy is celebrating its one hundredth anniversary this year - the Stanley Cup.

*115. The Château Frontenac slide,
1993 Photo: Brigitte Ostiguy*

Guests who were interested in something decidedly more romantic could opt for a sleigh ride through the streets of the city or along the Château boardwalk.

The Château's Ski Hawk School, which opened in the 1940s, launched many a promising career over the years and definitely contributed to the emergence of the Quebec City region as one of the most important downhill

117. The Château's dogsled team C.P.

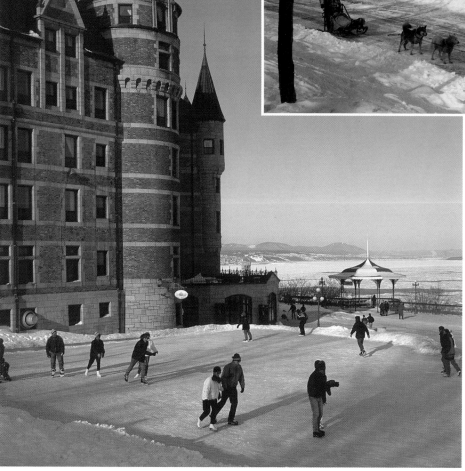

116. The skating rink, 1993
Photo: Brigitte Ostiguy

ski centres in North America. This ski school was directed for over ten years by the professional, Swiss-born ski pro and master of the "French Parallel technique", E. "Fritz" Loosli. Skiing classes were held at Lac Beauport, only twenty minutes by road from the Château. Day in and day out throughout the winter, enthusiasts took the 9:30 a.m. bus and headed for the ski slopes. The skiing classes were held from 10:00 a.m. to noon and 2:00 to 3:30 p.m. There was a ski chalet at the site where skiers could go for refreshments or to get warm. Afterwards, they all gathered at the hotel's Rendez-Vous Club.

Skijoring had its hour of glory in Quebec City too. Participants in skis were pulled by a car through the city, laughing merrily all the way and drawing envious looks from passersby as they returned to the Château.

*119. Skiing at the
Château C.P.*

*120. The Ski
Hawk School,
1945 C.P.*

Every year, one of the features of Winter Carnival is its famous canoe race across the ice-choked St. Lawrence. This exciting and traditional local event takes place literally right before the eyes of people at the windows of the Château. At the 1993 Winter Carnival, it was the canoe team supported by the Château Frontenac that won. Some people like to think that this was because of the hotel being in its centennial year, but actually it has won for three consecutive years and fairly often in the past. Still others talk about the legend of the *chasse-galerie*, being more inclined towards a supernatural explanation for the apparent ease with which the Château team beats the competition.

122. *The Château's canoe team, 1993*
C.P.

123. Quebec City's tercentennial, 1908 C.P.

Causes for Celebration

In 1908, Quebec City celebrated its three hundredth anniversary. To commemorate Samuel de Champlain's arrival on July 3, 1608, the Château Frontenac really put on the "ritz". Its imposing silhouette dominated a huge gathering of warships from three major world powers: Great Britain, the United States and France. At the foot of Champlain's statue, just a few feet from the Château, there was a grand ceremony to pay tribute to the founder of Quebec which was attended by the Prince of Wales, Vice-President Fairbanks of the United States and thousands of others.

On Thursday August 10 in 1916, the Château participated in an event that played an important part in the region's development: the official inauguration of Canadian Pacific's Gare du Palais train station, located in Lower Town just a few minutes away from the hotel. This official opening of the railway station, which from the outside was somewhat reminiscent of the already famous Château, took place just under one year after the cornerstone was laid on August 12, 1915.

The Château Frontenac organized the inaugural luncheon, a cold buffet presided over by the wife of Quebec City Mayor Lavigueur. Over two hundred of the three hundred people who had been invited were at the luncheon held in the main waiting room of the brand new railway station. This memorable banquet included cigars and cigarettes for the gentlemen and bouquets of flowers for the wives of important guests.

Quebec City owes much of its attraction as a tourist destination to the site on which it was built. This site would not have quite the same appeal, however, without the city's special culture and history. As the cradle of French civilization in North America, Quebec has become very popular over the years with English Canadian and American tourists, who appreciate its European-style charm.

124. The
Canadian
Folksong and
Handicrafts
Festival, 1930
*From Associated
Screen News.
Photo: Brigitte
Ostiguy*

French Canadian, or Québécois, culture has played an important part in many functions organized by the Château Frontenac. From May 24 to May 28, 1928, for instance, the Château hosted the Canadian Folk Song and Handicrafts Festival. This festival, which was under the auspices of the National Museum, National Gallery and Public Archives of Canada, gave French Canadian singers, musicians, story-tellers and craftspeople an opportunity to show off their respective talents. It was no small gathering either: festival directors Marius Barbeau of the National Museum of Canada and Harold Eustace Key, the musical

director for the Canadian Pacific, managed to talk the most celebrated concert performers and opera singers from Montreal, Toronto and the United States into taking part. One of these celebrities was the famous pianist and conductor Wilfrid Pelletier.

The shows included in the program were performed at the Château Frontenac, the Quebec Basilica and the Auditorium, as the Capitol Theatre was then called. The festival was a real tribute to French Canadian folklore and it drew the very best artists, who performed over six thousand songs, ballads and dances. Crafts also played a key role and there were demonstrations every day at the Château. Among other things, visitors were shown how to make a *ceinture fléchée*, the sash that was an essential element of traditional French Canadian dress.

125. *The return of
the Tall Ships,
1984*
Photo: Le Soleil

This festival was one of the most significant cultural events to be held at the Château in the late 1920s. The reputations of the participating artists went far beyond the bounds of the province, and the festival contest, with prizes worth a total of three thousand dollars awarded by Canada's Governor General E. W. Beatty, lent it an aura of fame all across Canada. The participation of the tenor Rodolphe Plamondon, pianist and composer Alfred Laliberté and professional singers Jeanne Dusseau and Cédia Brault - all celebrities - and of popular folk singers Madame Duquet and Madame Garneau, and the famous Ottawa quartet, the Troubadours of Bytown, with Charles Marchand, Émile Boucher, Fortunat Champagne and Miville Belleau, demonstrated how important folk music was at that time.

In 1930, the Château Frontenac held the Folk Dance, Folk Song and Handicrafts Festival. One of the highlights was a traditional country dance from the French province of Limousin performed by the *Disciples de Massenet* on Dufferin Terrace and directed by Charles Goulet.

In 1974, the Dufferin Terrace boardwalk vibrated to more exotic sounds - many of them African - created by artistic emissaries from French language countries gathered together for a huge French celebration, the *Superfrancofête*. In 1984, when the Tall Ships returned to Quebec, the wharfs at the foot of the Château were repaired and Quebec became a magical place. It was a moving sight as cruise ships and other craft came from all around to greet the Tall Ships against the backdrop of the historic old town and majestic Château.

Every year and every celebration brought its attendant festivities to lighten the hearts of the Château's guests. Originally the hotel was reserved for its guests only, but increasingly the local population adopted it for its own celebrations. The Château balls held particular appeal for the locals; they loved to dance under the stars and the northern lights, just as the hotel's guests did.

The Château Frontenac has always been noted for the excellent care it takes of its guests: its quality hotel service, fine food and all the little extras that keep people coming back. It also provides so many types of entertainment and things for guests to do that there is hardly any need for "homebodies" to leave the hotel!

127. *The Travel Exhibit, circa 1920 C.P.*

It can truly be said that the Château is a city unto itself. For a century now, there has always been something for everybody: shops, a music room, a newsstand, cocktail lounges, drawing rooms, a writing room, a library, a billiard room, an exhibition room and dance halls, to mention only a few.

Recreational Activities for all Tastes!

For the extroverted or sociable, the Château offered a billiard room, exhibition room, tea parties complete with music, dances, motion pictures, and parlour games such as the famous horse races held in the Jacques Cartier Room. The people of Quebec City used the Château Frontenace for their wedding receptions, graduation dances, meetings and other important functions.

128. *The dance floor of the Jacques Cartier Room, 1945 C.P.*

129. *Billiard room, 1925* C.P.

In the 1920s, the Travel Exhibit transported visitors to all the destinations served by the Canadian Pacific Railway with the help of photographs, cleverly displayed exotic objects and maps.

From time to time, movies would transform the Ballroom into a motion-picture theatre. During the 1956-1957 Christmas season, these films were among the fare offered to tempt movie fans: *Stormy, Lady Godiva, Country Girl, Happy Go Lovely, Bells of St. Trinians* and *Bridges of Toko-Ri.*

131. *Drawing for a pool table cover by W. S. Maxwell*
Maxwell Archives, CAC, Blackader-Lauterman Library, McGill

130. *New Year's Eve dance, circa 1940* C.P.

Music Aplenty

The Château Frontenac has always been a popular spot for musical appreciaton, singing, dancing and generally kicking up one's heels. Here too, there was something for all tastes: elegant concerts in the ballroom, more intimate chamber music recitals put on by the ladies' music club at teatime in the Salon Madeleine de Verchères, dances, and boisterous nightclub acts and variety shows in the Jacques Cartier Room.

One of the musicians who made a name for himself at the Château Frontenac was the multi-instrumentalist Pierre Marchand. He began his career there in 1919 as a cellist in the hotel orchestra conducted by J. R. Young, was made conductor in 1932, and began the following year to conduct the Château's eighteenth century quartet made up of two violinists, one cellist and one pianist. Between 1933 and 1950, Pierre Marchand gave over thirteen thousand concerts. The only times he did not perform were Good Fridays and the day King George V of England died!

132. The Château's eighteen century quartet C.P.

133. Teatime in the Palm Room, circa 1945 C.P.

Then there was Darisse: the regulars who used to haunt the Jacques Cartier Room in the fifties and sixties all remember Gilbert Darisse and his dance band, who performed every weekend.

Over the years, countless stars - singers as well as music hall and night club entertainers - have performed at the Château Frontenac, winning the hearts of generations of Quebecers and making the hotel a favourite for grand wedding receptions.

Many Quebec City families would not have missed the Christmas, Easter or Winter Carnival festivities at the Château for anything in the world. They were also very popular with Canadian and American guests, many of whom made a habit of coming back for them year after year. The magic surrounding these occasions was related and passed down from generation to generation, and it is not unusual to see the children and grandchildren of the hotel's early guests carrying on the tradition.

135. *Ballroom,*
1993
Photo: Brigitte
Ostiguy

136. **The menu**
for March 18,
1894 C.P.

Nectar and Ambrosia

Henri Journet, Louis Baltera, Christian Hitz, Oscar Hanselmann, George Gilhuber, Reynald Breton and Maurice Olaïzola are but a few of the renowned chefs who made the Château Frontenac a gastronomic mecca.

Right from the beginning, the Château's reputation for quality was closely linked to its fine food. The long list of menus offered over its century of existence, from the first cold buffet on a certain night in December of 1893 to the elegant repasts now served in its Champlain Room, is extremely impressive. Everyone, from the most humble and unknown of visitors to the most illustrious, was able to delight in its fine cuisine. All occasions were valid excuses for lavish displays of food fit for the gods: Christmas, New Year's Day, St. Patrick's Day, Hallowe'en, Easter, Winter Carnival, Mother's Day, conventions and visits by heads of state or movie stars would prompt the chefs and kitchen staff to turn the occasion into an unforgettable event. The artistic presentation and theatrical serving of the food was often brilliant in itself. For ceremonial dinners, the servants and chefs would file in with great pomp and pageantry bearing trays of aromatic delights. It was something to see when four "pages" carrying a colossal two hundred pound baron of beef marched into the ballroom to the accompaniment of the orchestra.

137. A 1922 menu
C.P.

*138. The board-
walk coffee-
house, circa
1920 C.P.*

The hotel kitchens were always an impressive bustle of activity. They have been known to hold almost two hundred people busy preparing a twelve-course banquet for five hundred guests. The chef obviously needed great coordination skills to manage this virtual army of workers.

Without any doubt, one of the Château's most remarkable chefs was Louis Baltera, who presided over its kitchens for more than thirty years. Baltera began his career as a very young man in the best establishments of Europe. North America beckoned, however, and after making a name for himself at the Netherlands Hotel in New York, he moved up the ladder via the Astor Hotel, Brooklyn's Crescent Athletic Club, then the legendary and chic Waldorf Astoria. In 1908, he was invited to the tricentennial celebrations in Quebec City; Quebec appears to have captured his imagination for he returned there for good in 1910, taking up his post at the Château Frontenac. Louis Baltera was a true artist and also an innovator: he raised the status of Quebec cuisine at

a time when it was looked down upon. His "Pea Soup, Habitant Style" and "Darne of Saguenay Salmon, Gaspésienne" reflected a creative sensitivity that enabled him to transform local culinary dishes into real masterpieces. Baltera's influence on the blossoming of fine dining in Quebec went well beyond the bounds of the Château.

Over its hundred years, the Château's chefs have worked hard to create and offer memorable dishes to the hotel's wide range of guests.

On September 6, 1894, some officers from the French Navy who had dropped anchor in Québec City enjoyed a ten-course dinner and some very fine wines. They must have been quite impressed by their repast and by the Château's obvious promise!

DÉJEUNER A LA FOURCHETTE

⁖⁖⁖

LE PRIX INDIQUE LE COÛT DU REPAS ENTIER

Jus de Tomate Rafraîchi

Consommé Julienne   Potage Mulligatawny

Soupe aux Pois, Habitant

———

Poisson Blanc du Lac Supérieur, Meunière, Tranches de Tomate 1.00

Rouget de Winnipeg Fumé Grillé au Citron, Cole Slaw 1.15

Omelette Créole avec Pointes d'Asperges Vertes .85

Hachi de Bœuf Salé Brun avec Oeuf Poché .95

Escalope de Veau Panée avec Spaghetti, Milanaise I 00

ROULANT CHAUD:- Baron d'Agneau Canadien Rôti, Sauce Menthe Fraîche 1.15

Pâté de Gibier Froid avec Salade de Fruits 1.00

Salade Chiffonade avec Oeuf Farci .75

———

Pois Verts Nouveaux   Purée de Navets

Pommes de Terre Mont d'Or ou Persillées

———

Pouding Sagou aux Pêches   Raisins   Tarte Epaisse aux Bleuets

Bavaroise aux Macarons   Fromage Kraft

Pomme Canadienne   Crème Glacée aux Fraises

———

Thé   Café   Lait

———

Servi dans la Grande Salle à Manger seulement

———

139. A 1939
menu C.P.

Forty years later, on June 22, 1934, the Consul General of Italy was the honoured guest at a special dinner which gave him the opportunity to savour the Château's fine cooking as well as its gracious hospitality: he was given a menu written in Italian and the wines and spirits served were from his homeland.

In 1939, the Château Frontenac was honoured by a royal visit from King George VI of England and Queen Elizabeth, the mother of the current monarch Queen Elizabeth II. Chef Louis Baltera truly outdid himself. On the evening of May 15, after the opening "God Save the King", there was a royal feast featuring, among other delights, a Crown Roast of Quebec Lamb and *Les Petits Oiseaux Blancs de l'Isle d'Orléans*.

Although the Château continued to serve delicious fare during the Second World War, a certain number of adjustments were made out of solidarity for the Allied cause. While the war raged on across the Atlantic, the hotel management demonstrated its sensitivity by suggesting that diners opt for something other than ham or bacon, citing the Dominion Department of Agriculture and Canadian Bacon Board recommendations to cut down on pork so that it could be sent to England, which was under siege. While we are on the subject of restrictions and observance of rules, it is interesting to note that the Château used to have a special fish menu for Lent. The one below most likely dates from the early 1950s.

"The CHATEAU FRONTENAC specializes in the cooking and preparing of fresh fish dishes particularly during the Lenten Season.

All our fish is expressed direct to us from the source of supply so that it is served to you with its natural fresh flavour.

These dishes have been tested by "Louis" our Chef de Cuisine and carefully selected to appease the palate of the most fastidious connoisseur."

140. Chef
J.F. Mots
Photo: Harvey
Lloyd

Stewed Oysters in Milk	.60
in Cream	.80
Baked Oysters à l'Ancienne or Bercy	.80
Fried Oysters with Tartar Sauce, Saratoga Potatoes	.75
Fresh Sea Scallops, Meunière, Sliced Tomatoes	.95
Broiled Live Lobster (Half)	
with French Fried Potatoes	1.60
Lobster Thermidor (Half) with New Green Peas	1.60
Fillet of Sea Bass, Amandine, Cucumber Rings	1.00
Broiled Bluefish with Anchovy Butter, Mexican Slaw	.95
Boiled Fresh Labrador Cod with Egg Sauce,	
Parsley Potatoes	.80
Steamed Alaska Smoked Cod with Drawn Butter,	
Boiled Potatoes	.85
Fresh Northern Lake Doré, Meunière, Rice Potatoes	.85
Jumbo Finnan Haddie Boiled in Milk,	
Boiled Potatoes	.80
Baked Fresh Halibut Steak, Créole, Boiled Rice	1.00
Fried Fillet of Lemon Sole, Tartar Sauce,	
Julienne Potatoes	.90
Fresh Haddock Sauté, Meunière, Tomato Salad	.80
Broiled Lake Trout with Cole Slaw,	
Long Branch Potatoes	.90
Fresh Lake Superior Whitefish, Spinach, Florentine	.90
Grilled Gaspé Pink Salmon with Sliced Cucumber,	
French Fried Potatoes	1.00
Fillet of English Sole, Marguery, Parisienne Potatoes	1.75
Boiled English Turbot, Hollandaise,	
New Green Beans	1.25

It goes without saying that observing Lent must have been quite a delicious affair with a menu like this one!

The relative "leanness" of the above dishes was in decided contrast with the traditional rich Quebec fare - chock-full of calories - listed on the leather-bound "Habitant Menu". Among other goodies, there were *cretons* served with bread toasted on the oven hearth, "Pea Soup, Habitant Style", "Pig's Feet Stewed with Meat Balls", steamed potatoes, young pickled beets and a mysterious pie called the *tarte à la Pichoune*.

Important religious holidays have always served as a pretext for special feasts and they gave the Château's different chefs over the years a chance to demonstrate their culinary talents. Needless to say, Christmas was celebrated with much pageantry, but there was also a special menu for Easter Sunday. In 1958, for instance, an elaborate Easter dinner was served to the sounds of music by Tchaikowsky, Chillermont, Waldteufel, Messager, Elgar, Puccini, Berlin, Paderewski, Gabrile-Marie and Friml, with Pierre Marchand conducting the orchestra. There was a mouth-watering selection of hors d'oeuvres, appetizers, soups, main dishes, vegetables and desserts that made choosing a difficult task. This six-course meal offered by Chef Christian Herz went for a staggering four dollars and twenty-five cents plus tax!

*141. **The new Salon Rose 1993** Photo: Brigitte Ostiguy*

Each decade brought the Château Frontenac its share of prestigious patrons. The 1960s were particularly fruitful, especially with all the heads of state and monarchs that Montreal's Expo 67 drew to the hotel. The chefs really had their work cut out for them that year and the Château's stoves never had a chance to cool down. One guest who called for especially good wining and dining treatment, what with the inevitable link between his country and matters of gastronomy, was the French President General de Gaulle. De Gaulle and his wife were at the Château on July 23, 1967, as the guests of the Quebec government. The splendid banquet in their honour was like something out of a dream: lobster tails accompanied by Cuvée des Écaillés riesling, quail served with Château Margaux wine, filet mignon washed down with Clos de Vougeot and, last but not least, parfait with Ernest Irroy champagne. Everything was sweetened with maple syrup in a happy marriage of two culinary traditions. This dinner did the Château proud, once more demonstrating its chefs' incredible knack for always coming up with just the right thing.

There have been many causes for celebration over the past three decades, the visits of Queen Elizabeth and President Ronald Reagan being two important occasions. Despite its distinguished, cosmopolitan clientele, however, the Château has always placed a great deal of emphasis on local tastes. In 1984, Chef Maurice Olaïzola invited Serge Bruyère, one of the most eminent chefs in Quebec City, to work with him on a menu for the "Presidents Dinner", an event organized to raise funds for the Quebec Symphony Orchestra. Some of the people who attended the function are still talking about the meal that resulted from the combined skills of these two virtuosos.

The perfectionism of its chefs was borne out with every meal that was served at the Château - even breakfast, the most important meal of the day. In the 1970s, apart from all sorts of à la carte possibilities, there were three breakfast combinations on the menu: the *Habitant* for two dollars and sixty cents, the *Regular* for two dollars and seventy-five cents, and the *Château* for three dollars and twenty-five cents. The *Habitant* included fresh squeezed orange juice; French toast made with the Château's own bread, and Quebec maple syrup; bacon; and coffee served in a large silver coffee pot. The *Château* was more typically British and consisted of fruit compote; cereal; two eggs with bacon, ham or sausages on the side; rolls, toast, buns or muffins with jam, marmalade or honey; and of course a big pot of coffee. The *Regular* included fresh fruit juice; cereal and cream; waffles with Quebec maple syrup; rolls, toast or buns with jam or honey; and coffee or tea.

The hotel's desserts were a pure delight to taste and behold. The local penchant for maple concoctions was often reflected on the menu offered to non-Quebecers. When they were in season, blueberries also added a bit of regional colour.

142. Château Frontenac poster, 1924 C.P.

143. **Guests
in the Jacques
Cartier Room**
*Photo: Brigitte
Ostiguy*

While we are on the topic of treats, another culinary tradition should be mentioned: various cheeses that are rarely found on North American menus. One of these is Oka cheese, which is also celebrating its centennial this year.

These few pages afford merely a glimpse of the Château Frontenac's fine food - a whole book could be written about its wine lists alone!

In this centennial year, the Champlain, the Café de la Terrasse and of course the ballroom are carrying on this tradition of excellence.

MOONLIGHT ON DUFFERIN TERRACE

QUEBEC
AND THE
CHATEAU
FRONTENAC

144. *Château Frontenac brochure, 1912 C.P.*

THE LEGEND

The Château St. Louis, under both the French and the English, was reputed for its superb interior decoration and for the elegance and splendour of its receptions. According to William Kirby in his novel *The Golden Dog*: "The great hall of the Castle of St. Louis was palatial in its dimensions and adornment. The panels of wainscoting upon the walls were hung with paintings of historic interest - portraits of the Kings, Governors, Intendants and Ministers of State, who had been instrumental in the colonization of New France". This was the backdrop for the seigniors' rendering of "fealty and homage" to the governor, important meetings of the Superior Council, and festivals of patron saints such as St. John the Baptist.

"A volume would not suffice to detail the brilliant receptions, gay routs, levees, state balls given at the Castle during Lord Dorchester's administration" (1786-1796), says James MacPherson Le Moine in one of his famous descriptions in *Picturesque Quebec*. He adds: "Unfortunately Quebec had then no Court Journal, so that following generations will have but faint ideas of all the witchery, the stunning head-dresses, the décolletees, high-waisted robes of their stately grandmothers, whirled round in the giddy waltz by whiskered, epauletted cavaliers, or else curtesying (sic) in the demure *menuet de la cour*" (*Picturesque Quebec*, p. 91).

145. Centennial celebration, 1993
Photo: Kedl

146. *Interior
    spaces in 1919.
    Postcard
    collection*
    *Maxwell
    Archives, CAC,
    Blackader-
    Lauterman
    Library, McGill
    University*

147. **Interior spaces in 1919. Postcard collection** *Maxwell Archives,
    CAC, Blackader-Lauterman Library, McGill University*

Nicolas Gaspard Boisseau attended the Queen's Ball given by Lord Dorchester on January 18, 1787. He describes the reception for us: "The Castle was filled with officers and notables from the city. There were many ladies present and they were a pleasure to behold indeed (...) Numerous servants offered refreshments as the hours passed by. At eleven thirty the dinner was laid out, with many pyramids of fruit, each one more succulent than the next. The dinner lasted an hour and a half, then Lord Dorchester stood up and withdrew. This did not prevent the ball from continuing on until five o'clock in the morning, however" (*Bulletin des recherches historiques*, Vol. XI, 1905 - Free translation).

On one "enchanted evening" two hundred years later, an extravagant reception took place on the same site. As in the past, the Château was ablaze with lights. Inside, there were flowers, lavish buffets and orchestra music to enchant the more than five hundred guests all decked out in their finery.

The *Le Soleil* newspaper of February 21, 1993 reported on this event worthy of Lord Dorchester and his cohorts: "The cooks, confectioners, cold cuts specialists and kitchen staff of the Château Frontenac did their utmost to satisfy the globe-trotting gourmets and epicures. Of the more notable delights on the menu, there were pyramids of shrimp, chilled and hot lobster, smoked salmon arranged in the shape of exotic fish, two delectable-looking turkeys, a *ronde de bison*, Bohemian pheasant, wapiti tourtière, caviar on buckwheat biscuits, *salami de bison*, maple taffy treats, *fraises au poivre*, and much more. Journalists came from Montreal, Ottawa, Toronto, the rest of Canada and all around the world to take part in this memorable culinary experience. Among the media represented were the *Folha* of Sao Paolo, Brazil, *Le Nouvel Observateur*, *Le Monde*, *Géo* magazine, the *Paris-Match*, the *Gault-Millau*, the Luxembourg radio and television network (RTL), the *New York Daily News*, the *Boston Globe*, the *National Geographic* from Washington, and the *NBC* network of Los Angeles. There were also members of the press from Japan, Germany, England, Italy and Switzerland" (Free translation).

The Château was all lit up for its centennial. William Van Horne's hotel had done itself proud and was showing off its splendid dining rooms, the panelling and warm hues of its halls, its chandeliers with their dancing reflections, its beautiful carpets, gilt ornamentation, mirrors, paintings and interior spaces which had been given a new lease on life for its one hundredth anniversary.

Regardless of any alterations yet to come, the Château retains its original spirit. One century of gracious living... This is the stuff of legends! A legend built on the magic memories and dreams of all those who have looked up at it at dawn, danced there under the stars and basked in its glow.

Once upon a time, there was a castle...

BIBLIOGRAPHY

Archives

Canadian Pacific Archives, Montreal

Archives nationales du Québec à Québec

Maxwell Archives, Canadian Architecture Collection, Blackader-Lauterman Library, McGill University

Microfilm

Graybill, S., Jr., *Bruce Price, American Architect, 1845-1903*, Doctoral thesis on microfilm, Yale University, 1957, McGill University Archives

Books

Choko, Marc H. and Jones, David L., *Canadian Pacific Posters 1883-1963*
Meridian Press, Montreal, 1988

Chambers, E. T. D., *The Guide of Quebec*
Quebec Daily Telegraph Printing House, 1895

Clouthier, Raoul, *The Lure of Quebec*
The Musson Book Co., Toronto, 1923

Gagnon Pratte, F., *Country Houses for Montrealers 1892-1924. The Architecture of E. and W. S. Maxwell*, Meridian Press, Montreal, 1989

Garceau, H. P., *Chronique de l'hospitalité hôtelière du Québec 1880-1940*
Éditions du Méridien, Montreal, 1990

Hart, E. J., *The Selling of Canada. The CPR and the Beginnings of Canadian Tourism*
Altitude Publishing, Banff, 1983

Kalman, Harold D., *The Railway Hotels and the Development of the Chateau Style in Canada*
Morris Printing Co., Victoria, B.C., 1968

Lamb, W. Kaye, *History of the Canadian Pacific Railway*
McMillan Publishing Co., New York, 1977

Lemelin, Roger, *The Plouffe Family*
McClelland & Stewart Ltd, Toronto, 1950

Le Moine, J. M., *Picturesque Quebec*
Dawson Brothers, Publishers, 1882

Morgan, Joan E., *Castle of Quebec*
J. M. Dent & Sons, Toronto, 1949

Noppen, L., Tremblay, M., and Paulette, C., *Québec: Trois siècles d'architecture*
Libre Expression, Québec, 1979

Pitcher, Rosemary, *Château Frontenac*
McGraw-Hill Ryerson, Toronto, c. 1970

Quebec Summer and Winter,
14th Edition, C.P. Railway Co., (April 1902)

Wylie, Evan M., *Canada's Castle in the Air*
Coronet, U.S.A., 1956

Periodicals

"Alterations and Additions to the Château Frontenac, Quebec, P.Q.", *Construction*, Vol. 18 (August 1925): 245-268

Ferree, Barr, "A Talk with Bruce Price", *The Architectural Record*, No. 5 (1899): 81

Henissart, Paul, "Le château sur le toit de Québec", *Sélection du Reader's Digest* (October 1981)

"Marché pour la construction du Fort de Québec", *Bulletin des recherches historiques*, Vol. VII (1901)

"Picturesque Château Frontenac Stands on Historic Grounds", *The Hotel Industry*, 1929, 3p

Price, Bruce, "A Large Country House", *Modern Architectural Practice*, No. 1 (1887): Preface

"Rebuilt Wing of the Château Frontenac", *Construction*, Vol. 19 (July 1926): 217-266

"The Beautiful Château Frontenac", *The Contractor* (May 1924)

Rogatnick, Abraham, "Canadian Castles. Phenomenon of the Railway Hotel", *Architectural Review* (1967): 364-372

Sturgis, Russell, "A Critique of the Architecture of Bruce Price", *The Architectural Record*, No. 5 (June 1899): 31

ACKNOWLEDGEMENTS

There are many individuals whose help and enthusiasm made this book possible. First of all, we would like to thank the people at Canadian Pacific Archives in Montreal: the archives assistant, Nancy Williatte-Battet, the archives manager, James A. Shields, and Stephen Lyons, Dan Holobow, Rick Robinson and David Hancock.

We would like to express our gratitude to our friends at of the Château Frontenac, and Gilbert Deschamps in particular. For their assistance during the writing stage, we are grateful to Danielle Hawey and Claude Sirard. Special thanks are due to Louise Mercier who did an excellent job as our production coordinator.

We are especially indebted to Brigitte Ostiguy for her enthusiam and superb photographs which bear such eloquent testimony to the beauty of the Château Frontenac, and to Linda Blythe for her fine translation which is a work in its own right.

Finally, we would like to emphasize the invaluable contribution of Joan Elson Morgan. It was her book *Castle of Quebec* which gave us the most pertinent descriptions of the Château Frontenac of Bruce Price's day.

The authors,

France Gagnon Pratte
and Eric Etter

Photographic Credits

Brigitte Ostiguy

Musée du Québec, Jean-Guy Kérouac, pp. 15 nᵒ 38; 19; 22 nᵒ 55; 56; 59; 76.

National Archives of Canada

Archives nationales du Québec à Québec, Livernois Collection

Archives nationales du Québec à Québec, E.-É. Taché Collection

McGill University, Canadian Architecture Collection, Maxwell Archives

Kedl

Ministère des Communications, Marc Lavoie

Ministère de la Culture, Inventaire des biens culturels du Québec

Gilbert Deschamps, Engineer

Arcop et associés

Château Frontenac

Canadian Pacific Archives

Abbreviations

NAC	National Archives of Canada
ANQQ	Archives nationales du Québec à Québec
IBCQ	Inventaire des biens culturels, Québec
C.P.	Canadian Pacific Archives